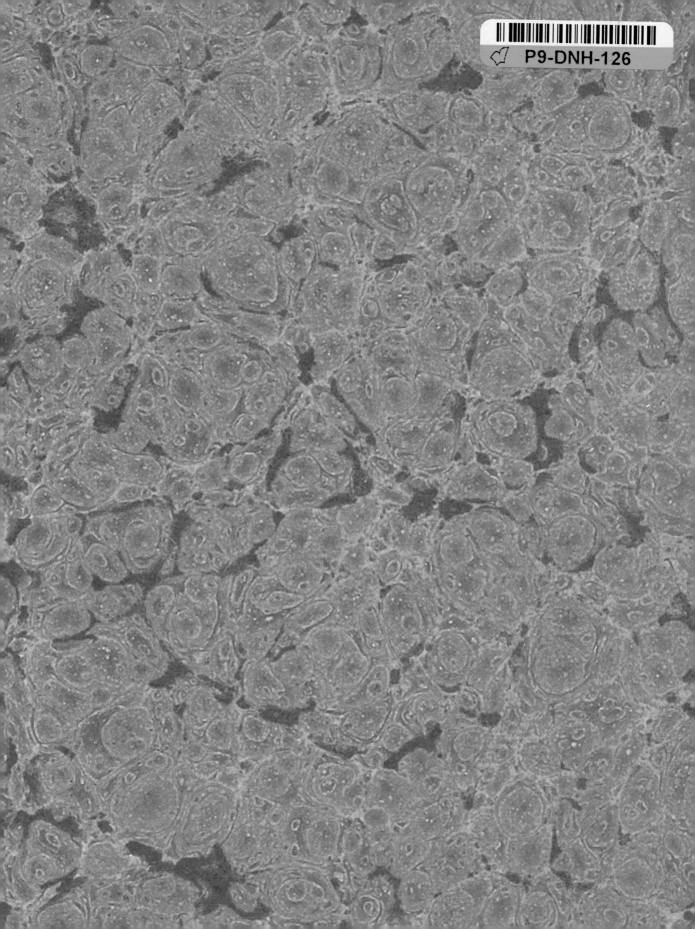

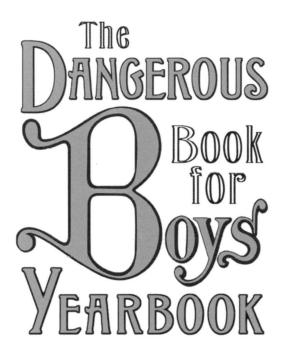

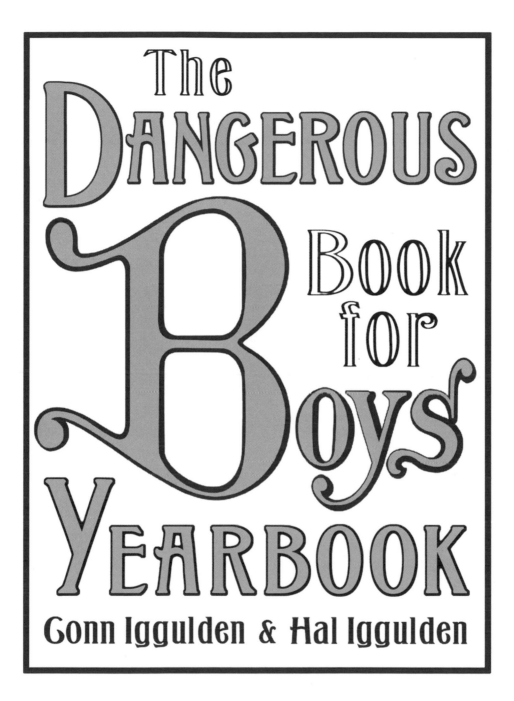

The Dangerous Book for Boys Yearbook

Conn Iggulden & Hal Iggulden

HarperCollins*Publishers*

HarperCollins*Publishers*
77–85 Fulham Palace Road,
Hammersmith, London W6 8JB

www.harpercollins.co.uk

Published by HarperCollins*Publishers* 2007
1

A catalogue record for this book
is available from the British Library

ISBN-13: 978 0 00 725539 9

Set in Centennial and Cheltenham by Jo Ridgeway

Printed and bound in Italy by
L.E.G.O. SpA - Vicenza

**At the back of the book, readers will find a full list
of illustrations, with a brief note in some cases on
the background.**

Introduction

With any luck, a Yearbook isn't just a way to plan a year, it's a way to record it. We really like the idea of stuffing news clippings and recipes into this one, and perhaps writing how proud you were to leave money under a child's pillow for his first tooth – remembering, of course, the cautionary tale of the child who slept with his head under the pillow, only to wake with a pile of coins and no teeth at all.

Without apology, it's a very British book. Given that the history of this island officially started with the arrival of Julius Caesar in 55 BC, you'll find Roman festivals in here, as well as hundreds of the characters and events that make this island such an odd place. Somehow, it only makes sense here that people go 'flounder tramping' in Scotland, or that the world conker championship takes place in Kent. It is sometimes astounding how many of these activities still survive. Many have died out, of course, which is not necessarily a bad thing. Sparrow Mumbling, or the game of trying to bite the head off sparrows tied with thread, is no longer popular. In addition, the practice of wife-selling has now fallen from its heyday. Yet there are new ones being invented, such as the Mad Maldon Mud Race, which began with a pub bet in the 1970s. Perhaps it's something in the water that brings these things into existence and then maintains them through centuries.

We've always loved history and facts. It's difficult to say why we like knowing when blackberries are ripe for picking, or that the man who collected dismembered pieces of Captain Cook in Hawaii was William Bligh, later captain of the *Bounty*. Perhaps it's a sense of controlling the world around us, or being part of it instead of just observers.

We hope you'll find something interesting in here for every day of the year to come – and we hope you'll add more from your own family. Births, deaths and marriages are worth putting in, of course, but you might also write a line or two about the people you meet, the parties or friendships you enjoyed, and perhaps the day you saw six magpies and could not remember the old rhyme. In that way, it will be your book as much as anyone's.

Conn Iggulden and Hal Iggulden

We have always enjoyed the remarkable range – and names – of saints, so on almost every day, we have noted our favourites. The phrase 'a red letter day', meaning an important or exciting day, comes from the practice of marking saints' days in red lettering on old calendars. You will find them in red here too.

SNOWFLAKES

Out of the bosom of the Air.

Out of the cloud-folds of her garments shaken,

Over the woodlands brown and bare,

Over the harvest-fields forsaken,

Silent and soft and slow

Descends the snow.

Even as our cloudy fancies take

Suddenly shape in some divine expression,

Even as the troubled heart doth make

In the white countenance confession,

The troubled sky reveals

The grief it feels

This is the poem of the air,

Slowly in silent syllables recorded;

This is the secret of despair,

Long in its cloudy bosom hoarded,

Now whispered and revealed

To wood and field.

Henry Longfellow

WINTER

Winter lasts in Britain from the solstice on 21 December to the vernal equinox on 20 March (occasionally falling on 22 December and 21 March). It's a time for heavier food, with lamb and beef somehow more suitable than they ever were in spring. They work well in a casserole or stew, with dumplings that 'stick to your ribs' and a bottle of red wine. Our father made a winter soup for many years, which never tasted the same twice as he put whatever ancient vegetables he could find in it, like parsnips, carrots, turnips and onions. As children, we complained bitterly at having to eat the soup, but when we look back now, yes we'll be forcing something similar on our own children. They need to grow too.

It's also a season to eat fatty birds like duck and goose, even if you prefer turkey at Christmas. Fish, too, can be just the thing at this time of year. Oysters and scallops are still available, as is cod and sea bass. Digging out a recipe for a fish pie is well worth doing, perhaps with a little Stilton cheese mixed in.

At this time, small children have gloves sewn onto lines of elastic. In theory this is so they are not lost. In practice it gives other children the chance to grab one and see how far it will stretch before snapping back or coming off. Ponds freeze and the days seem short, so that you rise in darkness and come home from work in the dark as well. It can be bitterly cold in Britain during winter, more so in Scotland and the north of England than the south. According to a Yorkshireman we once met, winter is when breaking down in your car in the middle of nowhere means you are in serious trouble.

Alcohol is a great comfort at this time and pubs are never more welcoming than

when you see the bright lights through the windows on a frozen night and hear the sound of talk and laughter inside. Smoky single-malt whiskies like Laphroaig go down very well in winter.

On the winter solstice itself, the sun is at its lowest point on the horizon all year. Daylight lasts between only seven or eight hours after the sun rises just after eight in the morning. It is literally the low point of the year, but from now on the days will lengthen, and although winter seems endless, spring is on its way.

Feasts and festivals in winter include: Christmas Eve and Christmas Day, New Year's Eve, or Hogmanay, the Mad Maldon Mud Race on New Year's Day, Epiphany or Twelfth Night on the 6 January, when the Magi arrived with gifts of frankincense, gold and myrrh, St Paul's Day on 25 January, known as Burns' Night in Scotland, The Clowns' Service in Dalston on the first Sunday in February, Candlemas on the 2 February, St Valentine's Day on 14 February, Shrove Tuesday (also known as Pancake Tuesday) before Lent, and Lent itself, which ends around the vernal equinox in March.

JANUARY

In Roman times this month was known as 'Januarius', named for the god Janus. He had two faces and so could look back at one year while looking forward to the next. In Roman mythology, he was the god of doors, which is a pretty poor lookout for a god.

The Romans originally had a calendar system of only ten months. They started well enough with Martius, Aprilis, Maius and Junius, but then ran out of ideas and numbered the months Quintilis, Sextilis, September, October, November and December – fifth, sixth, seventh, eighth, ninth and tenth. They didn't have months in winter, so the system worked fairly well for a time. Around the eighth century BC, a Roman named Numa Pompilius added January and February. No doubt the Romans would eventually have renamed the others, but they became very busy with an empire and never quite found the time before they were overrun by Vandals who cared very little for months.

There are many ancient superstitions and traditions associated with the New Year. Some households still open the back door at midnight to let the old year out, then open the front door to let the new one in. In parts of the country, the practice survives of opening a family Bible on New Year's Eve, hoping for some passage that can be read to mean good news in the months to come. If you attempt this, try not to open it at the Book of Revelation as it will dampen the mood somewhat. It's right at the end, so easy to avoid.

'First Footing' is the custom of welcoming the first person to cross the threshold on New Year's Day. Ideally, it should be a dark-haired man, carrying a piece of coal. This was once an important tradition in England and Scotland, though it survives primarily in Scotland today. Also in Scotland, Burns' Night remembers the poet Robert Burns with a haggis, poetry, speeches and a feast.

Despite January being one of the darkest, coldest months of winter, the New Year does bring a sense of renewal and hope, only slightly tainted by the suspicion that, somewhere close, others are having a better time than you.

PUNCH'S ALMANACK FOR 1897.

THE FIRST FOOT.

Enter Mr. Punch, who wishes everyone "A Merry Christmas and a Happy New Year!"

"The first foot in a house brings good or ill-luck for the year."—*Old Belief.*

BRADBURY, AGNEW, & CO. LD., PRINTERS, LONDON AND TONBRIDGE.

TRADITIONAL CUSTOMS

1 January, New Year's Day

The Mad Maldon Mud Race in Essex, which involves a 400-yard run across the River Blackwater and back. At low tide the race involves deep mud and raises thousands of pounds for charity each year.

The tradition of New Year water, also known as the flower or the cream of the well. Anyone who collects the first water drawn from any well, pond or stream on New Year's morning is certain of good luck for the coming year.

Mari Lwyd

Between Christmas and Twelfth Night in Wales, the ancient custom of Mari Lwyd takes place. 'Mari Lwyd' is usually said to mean 'Grey mare' or 'Grey lady'. It involves a wooden horse decorated with a real horse skull, coloured ribbons and white sheets – a symbol of fertility. The rider is led by five or six boys who also wear coloured ribbons and rosettes. In some areas, two of the band have blackened faces and are known as Punch and Judy. They knock upon a household door and cry out for permission to sing before being invited in. Inside, all manner of traditional tricks and treats take place, with the horse dancing around the house, nipping at the girls.

In the Glamorganshire version, each member of the band has a special name and a special task, like 'Merriman' who plays the fiddle, 'Judy' who sweeps the hearth, and 'Punch' who kisses the girls and is noisily chased by Judy. Food and drink is provided to all, and when time for departure comes they sing a traditional song calling down happiness and good fortune for the coming year.

Needle and Thread Ceremony, Queens College, Oxford
In 1341, Robert Egglesfield founded Queens College. He directed that on New Year's Day, every college student should receive from the bursar a needle with a coloured thread. To this day the bursar hands out the thread and needle saying to each student 'take this and be thrifty'. The whole ceremony is a pun in French on his name – 'Aiguille' and 'fil', or needle and thread, for Egglesfield.

6 January, Haxey Hood Contest, Lincolnshire
Haxey village in Lincolnshire stages the Haxey Hood Contest on 6 January. It commemorates the fact that Lady de Mowbray's hood once blew off and thirteen local labourers chased after it. She is said to have given each man half an acre on the condition that they re-enacted the event every year.

Nowadays, it involves the men of Haxey and the men of nearby Westwoodside struggling to bring a leather hood to one of two pubs in the area. Whoever catches it is surrounded by shoving groups, trying to push it in the direction they want. It is presided over by a 'Lord of the Hood', a Chief Boggin, ten minor Boggins and an official Fool. Both the Lord and the Chief wear hats decorated with flowers for the event. The Fool's face is painted black and red and his task is to make a speech of welcome while the Boggins light a bonfire behind him to 'smoke him' and stop the speech.

11 January, Burning the Clavie, Grampian

This is an old fire ceremony connected with New Year, running back into pagan antiquity. This festival took place in several fishing ports where flaming torches of fire were carried. The Clavie king and his band of young men built a bonfire on a cart using no manmade tools in a traditional fashion. At about six in the evening, burning peat is added to the bonfire and sets the whole thing alight. Tar is poured over it and the procession begins. It goes round the old town and young men take it in turns to be the Clavie bearer, pushing the cart. If one falls or stumbles it is very bad luck for him and the town. Eventually the procession reaches Doorie Hill, where the bonfire is left to burn all night and locals try to take bits of wood from it. These are considered lucky and a protection against evil for the New Year. Some are even sent overseas to the descendants of the village.

13 January, Old New Year's Eve

Before the adoption of the Gregorian calendar in 1752, New Year's Eve fell on the 13 January, It was marked with an old Pagan celebration in several east fishing ports where flaming torches of fire were carried.

14 January, Hunting the Mallard at All Souls College, Oxford

This ancient custom involves the Fellows of Oxford hunting a mallard around the college, accompanied by the Mallard Song. The event takes place only once a century and will not happen again until 2101.

17 January, Old Twelfth Night, Wassailling Orchards, Somerset

From ancient times, in the orchards of southern England, men gathered with cider and songs during Old Twelfth Night (which fell on the 17 January before 1752 and the Gregorian calendar). An ancient ritual was performed to protect the trees and the fertility of their crop from evil. Cider was poured over the roots of the finest tree and a piece of cake soaked in cider was laid at the foot of the tree with its lower branches also being dipped in cider. Then a toast was drunk to the tree and a charm was sung. To wassail a man was to drink to his health and prosperity.

27 January, Maids' Money, Guilford, Surrey

In 1674, John How left four hundred pounds to a charity now known as Maids' Money. The interest was to be gambled for using dice by two maids who had been in service for two clear years in the same household. The full amount of the interest was to go to the girl who threw the highest number. There was no money for second place.

In 1702 John Parsons left six hundred pounds with the interest to go to a maidservant of 'good repute'. This bequest became attached to John How's Maids' Money, and the girl who came second now received John Parsons' award, which has the interesting result of whoever comes last gets the most money.

29 January, 'Up Helly Aa', Lerwick, Shetland

This bonfire festival marks the end of the festivities of Yule, which in Northern Scotland lasts for 24 days. The tradition is for blazing tar barrels to be dragged by young men through the streets on wooden sledges. Each sledge contains four to eight barrels and is drawn by chains.

1 JANUARY

New Year's Day. Celebrated for the first time in 45 BC after Julius Caesar's reform of the calendar to 365 days. Our calendar is based on the slightly revised version created by Pope Gregory in 1582. On this day, Christ is said to have been circumcised.

Almachius, Fulgentius of Ruspe, Telemachus.

2 JANUARY

In 1757, during the Seven Years' War, Robert Clive, better known as Clive of India, captures Calcutta from the Nawab of Bengal, avenging the deaths of those who perished in the Black Hole.

Basil the Great, Gregory of Nazianzus, Caspar del Bufalo, Seraphim of Sarov.

3 JANUARY

In 1892, J. R. R. Tolkien (pictured below) is born.

Also on this day in 1946, the Nazi propagandist William Joyce is hanged for treason. Most famous for broadcasts to Britain during World War II that began 'Germany calling, Germany calling...', Joyce is better known as 'Lord Haw-Haw'.

 Genevieve.

4 JANUARY

In 1643, Isaac Newton is born in Lincolnshire, England. He becomes the leading mathematician of the age, formulating laws of motion and a new understanding of light and colour.

On this day in 1967, Donald Campbell is killed in the boat, *Bluebird K7*, attempting to break his own world speed record.

Elizabeth Seton - the first American to be canonised.

5 JANUARY

In 1531, Pope Clemens VII forbids King Henry VIII to remarry, indirectly leading to the formation of the Church of England.

 John Nepomucene Neumann, Simeon the Stylite, Telesphorus.

6 JANUARY

Twelfth Day. Epiphany. The Three Kings arrive. (Twelfth Night is actually the night before, on the fifth.)

On this day in 1066, Harold Godwinson is crowned King of England. He is later killed at the Battle of Hastings in October, after killing his brother Tostig at the Battle of Stamford Bridge. At Hastings, he is shot in the eye and then has to hold still for hours while the Bayeux Tapestry people finish their embroidery.

Also on this day in 1367, Richard II, son of Edward the Black Prince, is born.

Peter of Canterbury.

7 JANUARY

In 1610, Galileo discovers the four largest moons orbiting Jupiter, still known today as the Galilean moons.

Canute Lavard, Lucian of Antioch, Raymond of Penafort.

8 JANUARY

In 871 AD, King Alfred the Great triumphs over the invading Danes at the battle of Ashdown.

Abo, Gudule, Lucian of Beauvais, Severinus of Noricum.

9 JANUARY

In 1806, the funeral of Lord Nelson takes place at St Paul's in London. Having been preserved in alcohol for the voyage home, his body had been brought up the Thames the previous day, staying in the Admiralty overnight. The cathedral is hung with enemy banners captured at Trafalgar for the occasion. As the service ends, his coffin is lowered into the crypt, secure in an ebony coffin, where it remains to this day.

Adrian of Canterbury, Philip of Moscow.

In 49 BC, Julius Caesar crosses the Rubicon and begins a civil war.

On this day in 1863, the first section of the London Underground is opened from Paddington to Farringdon Street, the world's first underground railway.

Peter Orseolo.

In 1928, the novelist and poet Thomas Hardy dies. His family and friends disagree over what to do with his body. In the end, his heart is removed and buried all on its own in Stinsford in Dorset. The rest is cremated and the ashes taken to Poets' Corner in Westminster Abbey. His most famous works are *Tess of the d'Urbervilles*, *The Return of the Native* and *Far from the Madding Crowd*, among many other novels and poems.

Paulinus of Aquileia, Theodosius the Cenobiarch.

12 JANUARY

In 1879, the British initiate the Anglo–Zulu war, entering Zululand in South Africa. The battles of Isandlwana and Rorke's Drift follow shortly afterwards.

 Benedict Biscop, Tatiana.

13 JANUARY

In 1874, after the British retreat from Kabul in Afghanistan, the sole survivor of 16,000 men, women and children arrives at a British sentry post in Jalalabad.

Hilary of Poitiers. His name is behind the 'Hilary term' of Oxford University.

In 1878, Alexander Graham Bell demonstrates his invention, the telephone, to Queen Victoria. She is on it for hours.

Barba'shmin, Felix of Nola, Kentigern, who founded Christianity in Glasgow in the Seventh Century, Macrina the Elder.

On this day in 1790, Fletcher Christian and the Bounty mutineers land on Pitcairn Island in the Pacific and burn their ship in 'Bounty Bay'. They remain undiscovered until 1808, when an American whaling ship stops at the island.

Ita, Macarius the Elder, Paul the Hermit.

16 JANUARY

In 1809, General Sir John Moore dies at Corunna. The poem 'The Burial of Sir John Moore after Corunna' by Charles Wolfe is superb. It begins: 'Not a drum was heard, not a funeral note.'

On this day in 1920, the United States introduces Prohibition, making alcohol illegal. Instead of leading to a more orderly, peaceful society, the ban brings in huge revenues for the Mafia, helping to make organised crime a force in the country.

Otho, Peter, Accursio and Aiuto – the first martyrs of the Franciscan order, put to death in Morocco.

17 JANUARY

In 1946, the first session of the United Nations Security Council is held at Methodist Central Hall, opposite Westminster Abbey in London. The five permanent members are Britain, America, Russia, China and France. The other ten seats are temporary appointments for two years at a time.

 Antony the Abbot, Sulpice.

18 JANUARY

On this day in 1879, the first printing of the *Boys' Own* paper goes on sale.

 Margaret of Hungary, Prisca.

19 JANUARY

The feast day of King Canute, the King of all England, Denmark, Norway and bits of Sweden. His useless sons lost the lot after his death in 1035. Interestingly, the famous story about him holding back the waves has two versions. In one, his courtiers flatter him and he becomes arrogant enough to think he can hold back the tide – failing miserably. In the other, to demonstrate to those same courtiers that even a king has limits, he shows that he *cannot* hold back the tide. Given that the man was fantastically able and cunning, the latter story is probably the true version. He is buried in Winchester.

 Audifax and Abachum, who were martyred together, Canute IV, Henry of Uppsala, Martha and Wulfstan.

In 1936, Edward VIII, son to George V, ascends the throne, but abdicates before he is crowned, to marry Wallis Simpson. He dies without heirs and is buried in the same place as his great-grandmother, Victoria, at Frogmore in Windsor. It is worth noting that Edward VIII is buried in the gardens at Frogmore, where the rain can hit him.

 Euthymius the Great, Fabian and Sebastian who was shot with arrows, then battered to death.

In 1950, George Orwell (real name Eric Blair) dies. He was one of the greatest writers and thinkers of the twentieth century. His most famous works are *1984* and *Animal Farm*, though he was also a superb essayist and proponent of clear English.

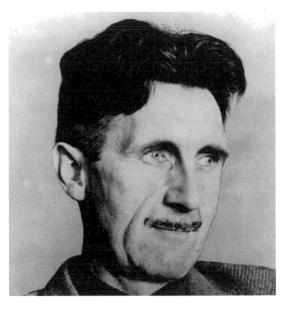

 St. Agnes, who died rather than give up her virginity, Fructuosus of Tarragona.

22 JANUARY

In 1788, the poet Byron is born in London.

On this day in 1879, the battles of Isandlwana and Rorke's Drift are fought. Eleven Victoria Crosses are awarded.

Also on this day in 1901, Queen Victoria, Empress of India, dies after 63 years on the throne.

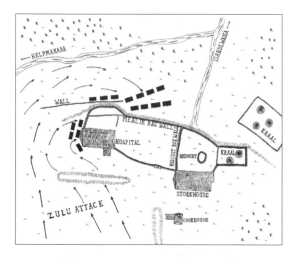

 Anastasius the Persian, Vincent of Zaragoza.

23 JANUARY

In 1571, The Royal Exchange in London is opened by Queen Elizabeth I.

On this day in 1989, the surrealist painter Salvador Dali dies.

 Ildefonsus, John the Almsgiver.

24 JANUARY

In 1965, Winston Churchill dies in London at the age of 90. St Paul's Cathedral, home to the tombs of Nelson and Wellington, is the venue for Churchill's state funeral six days later, most of which he planned himself.

On this day in 1536, Henry VIII falls during a joust and the horse rolls over him, leaving him unconscious. Though he later became enormously fat, he was very sporting right into his forties, and at this point had a 37-inch waist and a 45-inch chest.

 Francis de Sales.

25 JANUARY

Burns' Night. On this day in 1759, Robert (Robbie) Burns, the most famous Scottish poet, is born. In Scotland, his life is celebrated with a sumptuous meal centred around a haggis. Burns' famous poem 'To a Haggis' is quoted, beginning, 'Fair fa' your honest, sonsie face, Great chieftain o the puddin'-race!', before cutting the haggis.

On this day in 1924, the first winter Olympics is held. Unsurprisingly, the British have never done well in this event, lacking, as we do, snow.

Juventinus, Maximinus, Feast of the Conversion of St. Paul.

26 JANUARY

In 1788, having set sail from Portsmouth, British Captain Arthur Philip begins the first convict colony in Australia, landing at Sydney Cove on this day. The cove and the settlement (shown below) was named Sydney after the British Home Secretary Lord Sydney. This is now celebrated as Australia Day.

On this day in 1841, Hong Kong is ceded to Britain by China. It remains a British possession until 1 July 1997, the official closing date of the British Empire.

Finally, on this day in 1926, John Logie Baird, a Scottish inventor, gives the world's first demonstration of television in his attic to around fifty scientists. He would later achieve the first transatlantic transmission, the first live transmission in 1931 and the first demonstration of colour television.

 Alberic, Paula, Polycarp, Timothy and Titus.

27 JANUARY

In 1945, the liberation of Auschwitz by the Soviet army takes place.

Angela Merici.

28 JANUARY

In 1457, Henry VII, the father of the Tudor house that will produce Henry VIII and Elizabeth I, is born in Pembroke in Wales. He is buried in Westminster Abbey. His eldest son, Arthur, dies in 1502, allowing Henry VIII to become king.

Peter Nolasco, Valerius of Zaragoza and Thomas Aquinas, the brilliant philosopher and theologian of the Thirteenth Century.

In 1856, Queen Victoria signs a Royal Warrant to create the highest award for valour – the Victoria Cross. The medals themselves are still made today from cannons captured in the Crimea.

 Gildas the Wise, Sulpicius.

In 1649, the execution of King Charles I by Cromwell takes place. Charles I wears two shirts as it is a cold morning and he doesn't want the crowd to see him shiver and think he is afraid. He is allowed to walk his dog in St James's Park before the execution. When he is dead, the crowd pay to dip handkerchiefs in his royal blood.

On this day in 1948, Mahatma Gandhi is killed in New Delhi by a Hindu radical.

 Bathild, Martina.

31 JANUARY

In 1606, the Catholic conspirator Guy Fawkes is executed – hanged, drawn and quartered. He is one of the members of The Gunpowder Plot, an attempt to blow up the Houses of Parliament and assassinate King James I.

Aidan of Ferns, John Bosco, Marcella.

FEBRUARY

S·VALENTÍN·

This month is named after a Roman ritual of fertility and purification, or 'Februum'. On 15 February they would hold the great feast of Lupercalia. Among other things, it involved vestal virgins whipping naked men through the streets with strips of goat skin. Lupercalia may well be the true origin of St Valentine's Day. Some of the details are pretty racy for such a dull month, but it isn't as cold in Rome as it is in Britain. It might not seem quite so appealing in duffle-coats.

However, it's not all grim. On the first Sunday in February, the Clowns' Service is held in the Holy Trinity Church in Dalston, East London. Clowns from all over the world gather in full makeup and costume to commemorate the life of Joseph Grimaldi. He is considered the father of their profession and was born and died in London.

February is also the shortest month, with 28 days, or 29 in leap years. A leap year is when the number of the year is exactly divisible by four. Dates exactly divisible by 100 are exceptions. They are not leap years unless they are also divisible by 400, like the year 2000. It's a bit complicated, but there's nothing wrong with that.

Traditionally, women are allowed to propose to men on 29 February. The origin of the custom is unknown, though there is an apocryphal story about a conversation between St Bridget and St Patrick, where she complained that women could not ask men to marry them. He suggested that they could do so every seven years and she bargained him down to four. It is also traditional that if a woman is refused on this day, the man must buy her a silk gown.

Lent, the forty days of simple living before Easter, can begin from 4 February to 11 March. In earlier times, Lent was a period where no meat, eggs, fat or cheese would be eaten. It was abolished by the Puritans in the 1640s as they lived like that all the time and couldn't see the point. Charles II reinstated it, but it never had quite the same popularity as it had in previous centuries. It survives today in the widespread practice of 'giving something up' for Lent.

Shrove Tuesday, better known as Pancake Day, came from the attempt to use up all the food you weren't allowed to eat in Lent on the night before Lent began. The word 'shrove' is the past tense of 'shrive', which means confessing one's sins, so as to go into Lent with a spotless soul. With a little lemon and sugar, batter pancakes are delicious and well worth the effort. It is absolutely crucial that you try to flip one. They have been landing on floors and sticking to ceilings for centuries.

February is short and dark for the most part. For the Anglo-Saxons, February was known as Solmōnath – the 'mud month'.

TRADITIONAL CUSTOMS

Shrove Tuesday

On Shrove Tuesday, the women of Olney in Buckinghamshire run in a pancake race. The current
fastest time is 58.5 seconds.

Also on Shrove Tuesday, the company of
Marblers and Stonecutters meet at Corfe Town
Hall at noon. Apprentices become freemen at the
ceremony, after paying 33p, a penny loaf and two pots of beer. After that, they kick
a football from Corfe Castle to Owre, so it seems a custom that has all the necessary ingredients for a good day.

Hurling, St Ives

On the Monday nearest to 3 February, hurling takes place at St Ives in Cornwall.
This game is played on the beach, with the teams taken from two sides of the
town. The mayor holds the ball all year until the Monday morning, when he has
it blessed and then throws it to the players. The game ends at noon and the ball
is returned to the mayor for safe-keeping.

Candlemas Day

Candlemas Day, celebrated on 2 February, is the feast of purification of Our Lady
and the presentation of Christ in the temple. This is the tradition of blessing the
candles used in churches, which are then carried round in procession and given

out. It was celebrated back at least as far as the eighth century in Britain, though the name 'Candlemas' was not recorded before 1014.

Cradle-Rocking Ceremony, Blidworth, Nottinghamshire

On the Sunday nearest to Candlemas, an old wooden rocking cradle decorated with flowers and ribbons is placed in the church near the altar. The most recently baptised baby boy is laid in the cradle and rocked gently by the vicar during the service. Then the baby is restored to his parents and the service ends with the singing of 'Nunc Dimittis'. Held as far back as the thirteenth century in Blidworth, it was banned during the Reformation, revived in 1923, and has taken place every year since.

14 February/St Valentine's Day

St Valentine's Day has traditionally been the day for choosing sweethearts and giving love tokens. Chaucer, in the 'Parlement of Foules', refers to birds choosing their mates on 14 February. It was traditional to take the first person you saw on Valentine's morning as your Valentine and Pepys recorded in his diary in 1662 that Mrs Pepys kept her hands over her eyes all morning for fear of her first sight being the men working in her home. In Pepys' diary there are several entries concerning expensive Valentine gifts. Like many similar customs, this is a morning activity: the earlier the better.

1 FEBRUARY

In 1984 the half penny coin (pronounced hayp ny) is no longer legal tender, following the farthing, the sixpence, the shilling and the guinea into the history books.

Before 'decimalisation' in 1971, British coin values were based around the number twelve rather than ten. There were 12 pennies to a shilling and 20 shillings to a pound – so 240 pennies in a pound. A guinea was a pound and a shilling – so 21 shillings. Guineas survive today in certain high price areas such as the sale of racehorses. In those auctions, it is possible to bid in pounds and have someone shout 'Guineas' to top the bid.

Shillings and pennies were originally silver coins. Shillings were introduced in 1504 and pennies much earlier, perhaps back to the fifth century and the withdrawal of Rome. In 'old' money (before 1971), pennies were written with the symbol 'd' which stood for *denarius* – a Roman silver coin.

The reason British money is called a pound is because 240 silver pennies weighed 12 ounces – the exact weight of a Roman pound. It is also interesting to know that the '£' symbol is a short form for the imperial weight measurement of a pound 'lb', which stands for the Latin word for pound, *libra*.

 Brigid, Pionius.

2 FEBRUARY

On this day in 1943, the German 6th Army surrenders at Stalingrad after months of some of the most vicious fighting of World War II.

For centuries in Scotland, this was the first Quarter Day of the year, when rents were due. Although it was not an official Quarter Day in England, it remained a day for settling accounts and debts right up to the twentieth century. The second Scottish Quarter Day is on Whitsunday, the seventh Sunday after Easter.

 Joan de Lestonnac.

3 FEBRUARY

In 1966, the first soft landing of an unmanned probe on the moon is achieved by the USSR. The probe is named *Luna 9*. This Soviet success spurs America on in the race to put a man on the moon. A previous American probe, *Ranger 8*, crashed into the moon in 1965, as it was designed to do, sending back 7,000 pictures before impact. However, the soft landing of *Luna 9* showed that one day a manned landing might be possible.

 Blaise, Ia, Lawrence of Canterbury.

In 1789, George Washington is elected as the first President of the United States.

Gilbert of Sempringham, Joan of France, John de Britto, Phileas.

The Prince of Wales (who will later be George IV) becomes Prince Regent after his father, George III, is certified as insane. He was not one of the great romantic lovers of history. He married Caroline of Brunswick in 1795 only because parliament agreed to pay his debts if he did. When the Prince finally consummated his marriage, he felt ill and had to be given brandy.

Agatha, patron saint of bell-makers.

6 FEBRUARY

In 1952, George VI dies in his sleep at Sandringham House aged 56. His daughter becomes Queen Elizabeth II. He is buried at St George's Chapel, Windsor

On this day in 1971, Alan Shepard, the American astronaut, plays golf on the moon at the end of the Apollo 14 mission, hitting the ball 'miles and miles and miles'. It was the longest golf drive in history until 22 November 2006, when Russian Cosmonaut Mikhail Tyurin hit one from the International Space Station. That ball is still orbiting.

 Dorothy, Martyrs in Japan, Photius.

7 FEBRUARY

In 1812, Charles Dickens is born in Portsmouth. He becomes one of the great names in literature. His most famous works include *Oliver Twist*, *David Copperfield*, *A Tale of Two Cities*, *Great Expectations*, *Nicholas Nickleby* and *A Christmas Carol*.

Theodore the General.

8 FEBRUARY

In 1516, Mary I is born at Greenwich Palace – daughter to Henry VIII and Catherine of Aragon. After the death of her half-brother, Edward VI, she is next in line to become queen of England and Ireland. A devout Catholic, the struggle between 'Bloody Mary' and her equally ruthless sister Elizabeth will tear the realm apart in religious war. Though married to Philip II of Spain, she has no heirs and so paves the way for her sister to come to power.

 Cuthman, Jerome Emiliani, John of Matha.

9 FEBRUARY

In 1983, Derby winner Shergar is stolen in County Kildare. The horse is never recovered. It has long been thought that Shergar was kidnapped by the IRA and held for ransom, but then broke a leg in captivity.

Apollonia, Nicephorus of Antioch, Teilo.

10 FEBRUARY

In 1763, the Treaty of Paris is signed, ending the Seven Years' War – the real World War I, and by far the most successful war ever fought by Britain, as it brought India and Canada into the fold, denying those territories to France. The French nearly won it all back with Napoleon, of course, but 'nearly' is quite important in these matters.

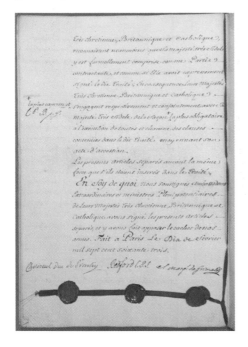

 Scholastica, the twin sister of St. Benedict.

11 FEBRUARY

In 1940, John Buchan dies. He was a Scottish novelist responsible for classics such as *The Thirty-Nine Steps* and *Mr Standfast*. He became Governor General of Canada. His ashes are buried in Elsfield, near Oxford.

Benedict of Aniane.

12 FEBRUARY

In 1809, Charles Darwin is born. At the age of only twenty, he takes part in a scientific expedition on HMS Beagle to South America and, most famously, the Galapagos islands, off the coast of Ecuador. There, Darwin finds giant tortoises and iguanas that have evolved differently in the isolated islands. He also finds species of birds unique to the islands. After returning to England, he goes on to write *The Origin of Species* and formulate the theory of evolution. One of the greatest minds of the nineteenth century, he is also one of the last scientific non-specialists: a naturalist, biologist, geologist, author, illustrator, taxidermist and medical student.

Julian the Hospitaller, Marina.

13 FEBRUARY

In 1692, the Glencoe Massacre takes place. Thirty-eight Macdonalds are killed by Campbells they have taken in as guests. Forty more women and children die of exposure after their homes are burned.

 Catherine dei Ricci.

14 FEBRUARY

St Valentine's Day. Evolved from 'Luper-calia', a racy festival in the Roman calendar where pretty much anything was allowed. St Valentine was a priest who married Christian couples and so disobeyed the Roman emperor, who had forbidden soldiers to marry. Valentine was beheaded on this day in 270 or 271 AD.

On this day in 1779, Captain Cook is killed by Hawaiian islanders. Originally he and his crew were welcomed as gods, until one of them died, giving the game away. The native islanders took a dim view of the deception. One of the men who collects Cook's dismembered body parts is William Bligh, most famous for the later mutiny on the Bounty.

Cyril and Methodius. Most famously, this is St. Valentine's day.

15 FEBRUARY

In 1971, decimal currency is introduced in Britain for the first time. Sixpences remain legal tender until 1980.

 Claude La Colombière, Sigfrid.

16 FEBRUARY

In 1937, Nylon, a synthetic polymer, is patented by DuPont after work by Wallace Hume Carothers. It is later used for stockings and is therefore a very good thing indeed.

 Elias, Jeremy, Isaias, Samuel and Daniel – martyred together in Palestine.

17 FEBRUARY

In 1909, the Apache leader Geronimo dies at the age of 80. Geronimo was actually a nickname given to him by Mexican soldiers. His real name was Goyaalé, sometimes spelled Goyathlay. It means 'yawner'. He led the last major force of Native American Indians in resistance against the white settlers, finally surrendering in 1886. His daring exploits meant that the name Geronimo became synonymous with wild bravery. It is still shouted today by parachutists and anyone else attempting something dangerous.

 Finan, Fintan of Cloneenagh, one of the Seven Founders of the monastic Servite Order, which survives today.

18 FEBRUARY

In 1930, Pluto is discovered by American Astronomer Clyde Tombaugh. Even today, the argument rages about whether it can be classed as a planet. It does not orbit the sun on the same plane as the other planets, sometimes even coming closer in than Neptune, the eighth planet. However, Pluto is big enough to be spherical (as opposed to irregularly shaped asteroids) and it also has a moon, 'Charon'. We think it's a planet.

Colman of Lindisfarne, Flavian of Constantinople.

19 FEBRUARY

In 1473, the astronomer Nicolaus Copernicus is born. His understanding of the solar system will overturn the idea that the universe revolves around the earth. It seems a little obvious now, but he was the first to describe the planets spinning around the sun.

 Mesrop the Teacher.

20 FEBRUARY

In 1947, Lord Louis Mountbatten becomes the last Viceroy of India, helping to accelerate the independence of Pakistan and India from British rule. Mahatma Gandhi calls the process 'the noblest act of the British Nation'. Mountbatten, a hero of World War II, is later killed by an IRA bomb in 1979.

 Shahdost, Ulric of Haselbury.

21 FEBRUARY

In 1952, restored to the position of Prime Minister after the post-war government of Clement Attlee, Winston Churchill permanently abolishes ID cards.

 Peter Damian, an 11th Century monk and theologian.

22 FEBRUARY

Date of the ancient Roman festival of Caristia, worth mentioning as it is the one where all family quarrels are forgiven. Also known as Cara Cognatio.

Margaret of Cortona.

23 FEBRUARY

In 1863, British explorers John Hanning Speke and J. A. Grant announce they have found the source of the river Nile, astounding the people living there.

 Mildburga, Polycarp.

24 FEBRUARY

In 1971, Conn Iggulden is born.

On this day in 1981, Prince Charles and Lady Diana become engaged, stealing the thunder on Conn's tenth birthday.

 Montanus and Lucius.

25 FEBRUARY

In 1723, Sir Christopher Wren dies at the age of 91, the greatest architect of his time. As well as St Paul's Cathedral, he designed the Monument to the Great Fire of 1666, the Royal Observatory at Greenwich and the library at Trinity College, Cambridge, as well as more than fifty other churches and secular buildings. He is buried in St Paul's under the words: '*Lector, si monumentum requiris, circumspice*'. ('Reader, if you seek his monument, look around you.')

Ethelbert of Kent, the Anglo-Saxon King who welcomed St. Augustine and builder of the first cathedral of St. Paul in London.

26 FEBRUARY

In 1987, the Church of England synod says yes to women priests.

On this day in 1993, the World Trade Centre in New York is bombed, killing five people.

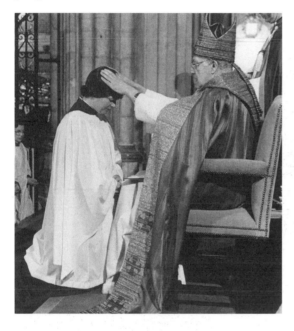

 Porphyry of Gaza.

27 FEBRUARY

In 1815, Napoleon escapes from the Island of Elba, beginning the Hundred Days' War, which ended at Waterloo.

Gabriel Possenti, Leander.

28 FEBRUARY

In 1900, the Relief of Ladysmith takes place, during the second Boer war in South Africa. British forces were besieged by the Dutch Boers for 118 days and lost almost 200 dead. On this day, the British commander, Lieutenant General George White, greets the relief force with the words, 'Thank God we kept the flag flying.'

On this day in 1948, the last British troops leave India.

Oswald of Worcester, Martyrs of the Plague at Alexandria.

29 FEBRUARY

An extra day, included to reflect the fact that each year is longer than 365 days. In fact, a year is 365.242190 days long, or, more roughly, 365 and a quarter. Four quarters make an extra day every four years – except for centuries, unless they are divisible by 400. Therefore, 2000 was a leap year, but 2100 won't be. People born on 29 February only have a birthday every four years, though they usually cheat shamelessly and have an undeserved birthday party on a different day.

 Oswald, Cassian.

MARCH

This is the month that is said to 'come in like a lion and go out like a lamb'. In other words, it can still be windy and freezing at the beginning, but by the end, spring arrives and winter is gone for good. The vernal equinox comes on 21 March, a day of equal light and dark as the world swings around the sun to the point where the northern hemisphere gets more and more light. Clocks go forward on the last Sunday in March, marking the beginning of British Summer Time.

March is named from the Roman month 'Martius', after Mars, the god of war. With flowers pushing their way up through the hard ground, and spring in the air, there is, after all, no better time to go to war. The second Gulf War started on 20 March 2003 and the NATO bombing of Kosovo commenced in March 1996.

If war is too much trouble, March is a planting month, unless the ground is still frozen. Grass grows at 42°F (6°C) and above, so if your grass is growing, anything else will too. Find a few potatoes with small shoots showing. The official term is that they have 'gone to seed'. Any you plant in March to April can be harvested around thirteen weeks later. You could then replant some of those to dig up in September. It is ridiculously satisfying to do this, and potatoes produce an impressive crop. Even in a tiny patch of a garden, you can get a few meals' worth. Resist the temptation to dig them up and see how things are going.

Radishes are marvellously spicy to taste and have the advantage of growing quickly and providing multiple crops. Nothing is easier to grow in a garden. You can plant those from March until as late as July. Seed packets can be bought at any garden centre. Sow them two inches apart and about half an inch down. You'll harvest the crop about six weeks later. Honestly, if you've never done it, it's worth clearing a patch of weeds and having a go – especially if you have children for the heavy labour.

Finally, March is also the last pruning month. If you have roses, blackberries, raspberries or loganberries, cut them right back. Be ruthless – they'll return with a vengeance. Blackberries are very hardy, while loganberries and raspberries need a sheltered place and, ideally, some sort of support frame for them to grow.

TRADITIONAL CUSTOMS

Commonwealth Day

Commonwealth Day is on the second Monday in March. It replaced Empire Day on 24 May, when the Empire was mislaid.

1 March, Whuppity Stourie

In Lanark, Scotland, this old spring custom begins with the ringing of the town bell in the parish church. Crowds of people gather with the Provost outside the church at 6 p.m. Each child carries a homemade weapon of a ball on a string. As the bell rings, they circle the church three times, beating each other with their weapons. Then the provost throws ten pounds' worth of pennies, which the children gather up while he gives an address to the crowd. An older custom is called 'buffing the bell-man'– as they ran around the church they would try to hit the bell and the bell-ringer. Then they would all run off to Wellgate Head to meet the young men of New Lanark for a fight. The bell-ringing is intended to welcome the spring and as a commemoration of a former custom of whipping penitents around the church. In this custom, there are visible remnants of more ancient magical rites where winter is fought, defeated and finally driven from the land.

Cheltenham Festival

The Cheltenham Festival of Jump Racing takes place from 13 to 16 March each year, with the Gold Cup being run on the last day. Three million pounds in prize money is at stake over the four days, with crowds limited to 55,000 or 65,000 for the Gold Cup itself.

Boat Race

In the last week of March, or early April, the Oxford and Cambridge Boat race takes place. The tradition began in 1829, when two friends at Harrow school separated at university. Charles Merivale at Cambridge sent a challenge to Charles Wordsworth at Oxford (nephew of the poet William Wordsworth). The first race was run, and even back then 20,000 people turned up to watch. Today, a quarter of a million people line the banks of the Thames, and the event is televised with an audience of more than eight million.

31 March, Oranges and Lemons Ceremony, St Clement Danes, London

When oranges and lemons first came to England in the Middle Ages they were taken up the Thames by barge and landed close to the churchyard of St Clement Danes in London. They paid a toll at Clements Inn on their way to Clare Market. The modern ceremony started in 1920 when the bells of the church were made safe and re-dedicated. The children from a nearby primary school joined in for a short service in which the traditional nursery rhyme was sung and oranges and lemons were given to the children. This was observed until the outbreak of World War II, when the bells were damaged again. In 1957 the bells were re-hung and the famous nursery rhyme is still played four times a day at nine o'clock, noon, three o'clock and six o'clock on 31 March.

1 MARCH

St David's Day. The Patron Saint of Wales, St David is known there as 'Dewi Sant' or St Daveth. Legend has it that he was the uncle of King Arthur. He is also said to be the one who came up with a leek as a Welsh symbol, to distinguish their soldiers on the battlefield.

Also on this day, the trout-fishing season begins.

 David, Swithburt, Rudesind.

2 MARCH

In 1791, John Wesley dies. He was the founder of Methodism, an evangelical aspect of the Church of England. As a result of his influence, there are Methodist churches all over the world. His brother Charles is author of some of the greatest hymns ever written. John Wesley is buried in Wesley's Chapel, London.

On this day in 1969, Concorde flies for the first time, the result of an Anglo–French project to create a supersonic passenger plane that somehow ends up with the French spelling.

 Chad, pupil of St. Aidan and brother to St. Cedd.

3 MARCH

In 1539, Sir Nicholas Carew is beheaded. His is a forgotten story, but he was once a favourite of King Henry VIII and a very accomplished knight. He was present at 'The Field of the Cloth of Gold', Henry VIII's meeting near Calais with the French king. At the jousting on that day, Carew was successful against all-comers and not unhorsed. He was a distant relative of Anne Boleyn and also jousted successfully at her coronation. The story goes that when Henry VIII spoke rudely to him at a game of bowls, Carew forgot caution and replied in the same manner, deeply offending the king. Eventually, he was charged with exchanging letters with Exeter, a traitor. Carew was executed at Tower Hill, London.

Aelred, Cunegund, Marinus of Caesarea.

4 MARCH

In 1941, Operation Claymore takes place. A British commando expedition attacks Nazi facilities in the Lofoten Islands in Norway in an attempt to capture an Enigma code machine. They destroy eleven factories, 800,000 gallons of oil, sink 18,000 tons of shipping and find Enigma machine parts and code books. They capture 228 German prisoners and return with more than 300 loyal Norwegians. In the process, they take only one wound, an accidentally self-inflicted cut to the thigh.

 Casimir.

5 MARCH

In 1133, Henry II is born at Le Mans in France. Later, he becomes King of England as well as parts of France – Normandy and Aquitane. He fathers four sons, including two who go on to rule: Richard I and John. Henry is buried in France at Fontrevault Abbey.

Ciaran of Saighir, Phocas of Antioch, Piran.

6 MARCH

In 1475, Michelangelo di Lodovico Buonarroti Simoni is born in Tuscany. He will go on to produce the greatest sculptures and paintings in history. His most famous work is perhaps La Pieta, a sculpture of Mary holding the body of Jesus across her knees. He is also famed as the painter of the Sistine Chapel in Rome, for his statue David and numerous other works. He was a Renaissance man in the literal sense of living in the Renaissance period, but Michelangelo was one of those who led to the term meaning 'skilled in many arts'. An architect, sculptor and painter, he lived at the same time as Leonardo da Vinci. Both men disliked each other intensely, which is perhaps not too surprising.

 Chrodegang, Colette, Cyneburga.

7 MARCH

In 1810, Admiral Lord Collingwood dies. Born in Newcastle, he was a great friend of Nelson and their tombs lie in the same section of the Undercroft in St Paul's Cathedral. It was Collingwood who fired the first shot at Trafalgar in 1805, prompting Nelson to say 'See how that noble fellow Collingwood carries his ship into action!' Collingwood took command on Nelson's death. He met Nelson first in Jamaica, when they were both midshipmen. They were friends ever after. Before battle was joined at Trafalgar, Collingwood received Nelson's famous signal 'England expects that every man do his duty'. He said aloud: 'What on earth is Nelson signalling about? We all know what we have to do.'

NELSON'S SIGNAL AT TRAFALGAR.

 Paul the Simple, Perpetua, Felicity.

8 MARCH

In 1702, William III dies after his horse stumbles on a mole-hill at Hampton Court. On this day, Catholics in Ireland raise a toast to 'the little men in velvet jackets' – the moles responsible for his demise. As William III has no heirs, the line passes to Queen Anne, daughter of James II and Anne Hyde. When she too dies without heirs, after *17* children dying in infancy and one dying aged eleven from 'too much dancing', the Hanoverian line begins with George I.

On this day in 1917, the Russian revolution begins, leading to the abdication of Tsar Nicholas II on 16 March and his execution along with his family. From these grim events, the USSR is formed, which lasts for 74 years until 1991.

 Felix of Dunwich, John of God, Julian of Toledo, Senan of Scattery.

9 MARCH

In 1862, the Battle of Hampton Roads takes place, the first battle between iron-clad ships. It is fought between the USS *Monitor* and the CSS *Virginia* as part of the American Civil War. Wooden ships could not stand such firepower anywhere near as well, and after this battle the ship-building nations such as Britain and Germany raced to create fleets of 'iron-clads'.

Catherine of Bologna, Frances of Rome, Gregory of Nyssa.

10 MARCH

In 1876, Alexander Graham Bell sends the world's first telephone message to his assistant Thomas Watson. The spectacularly uninspiring words are: 'Mr Watson, come here. I want you.'

 John Ogilvie. Also, the forty martyrs of Sebastea – all members of the XIIth Roman legion 'The Thundering Legion' who refused to renounce Christianity. They were stripped naked and frozen to death on an icy pond. Only one man gave in and his place was taken by another who had been impressed by the example of the others.

11 MARCH

In 1955, Alexander Fleming, the discoverer of penicillin, dies of a heart attack, aged 73. Also on this day, in 1988, the pound note ceases to be legal tender.

Eulogius of Cordoba, Sophronius.

12 MARCH

In 1999, violinist Yehudi Menuhin dies while in Berlin. He was one of the great musicians of the twentieth century. Born in New York, he performed as a child prodigy in London, Paris, Berlin and San Francisco, and, later, for the allied troops during World War II. He spent most of his career based in Britain, making a permanent home there in 1985. He was made a life peer, Baron Menuhin, in 1993.

Maximilian, Paul Aurelian, Simeon the New Theologian.

13 MARCH

In 1764, Charles Grey, the second Earl Grey, is born. Later, he would make popular the flowery blend of tea and bergamot orange oil that still bears his name. The exact origin of the blend is unknown, but it may have been a gift when the Earl was Prime Minister in the 1830s. There is a story that one of Earl Grey's men saved a Chinese Mandarin's son from drowning and the tea was given to him as a result. The tea company Twinings managed to make up a blend from the original and marketed it as Earl Grey's Tea.

Euphrasia, Gerald.

14 MARCH

In 1879, the theoretical physicist and mathematician Albert Einstein is born. He is best known for his theory of relativity and influence on the Manhattan Project, which led to the first atomic bomb. Einstein was a Nobel Prize winner and his name has become synonymous with genius. Unusually large head.

Matilda.

15 MARCH

This date was known on the Roman calendar as the Ides of March. On this day in 44 BC, Julius Caesar is assassinated, in Pompey's theatre, Rome.

Clement Hofbauer, Leocritia, Louise de Marillac.

16 MARCH

In 1912, Captain Lawrence Oates steps out into a blizzard near the South Pole with the words 'I'm going out, I may be some time'. He knew he had reached such a state of physical collapse that he could only be a hindrance to the others and lessen their chance to survive. His body has never been found.

Herbert of Cologne, Julian of Antioch, The Martyrs of North America - eight French-born Jesuits killed in the 17th century as they tried to bring Christianity to the Native American tribes.

17 MARCH

St Patrick's Day, patron saint of Ireland.

The day is also dedicated to Saint Joseph of Arimathea, who laid the body of Jesus in the tomb. Shrouded in legend, his life is worth inclusion as he is said to have been a tin merchant who travelled to Cornwall and Glastonbury – possibly with a young Jesus in tow. That legend is behind the words of Blake's hymn 'Jerusalem', beginning 'And did those feet, in ancient time, walk upon England's mountains green?'

On this day in 1834, the six 'Tolpuddle Martyrs' are sentenced to hard labour and transportation to a prison colony in Tasmania. They had formed an early Trade Union, 'The Friendly Society of Agricultural Labourers'. The local landowner complained about them to the Prime Minister and they were arrested, found guilty of an obscure law concerning oath-giving and deported. After a public outcry, all six were released.

Gertrude of Nivelles, Patrick, Joseph of Arimathea.

18 MARCH

In 1745, Robert Walpole dies. Although the position was not created until later, he is recognised as Britain's first and longest serving Prime Minister. King George II spoke no English and could communicate to his parliament only through Walpole who sat next to him and spoke fluent German. He was the first Prime Minister to reside at 10 Downing Street, the house a gift to him by a grateful George II.

Cyril of Jerusalem, Edward the Martyr, Salvator of Horta.

19 MARCH

In 1821, Richard Francis Burton is born in Devon, an extraordinary character by anyone's standards. As well as a successful army career, where he served in India as a captain, he travelled in disguise to Mecca, aided in the deception by an astonishing command of more than twenty languages and dialects, including Hindustani, Gujerati, Persian and Arabic. He had himself circumcised so that he would not be given away. He was a consul in Damascus, a spy, a superb fencer and a man often at odds with the moral aspect of Victorian society. Later, he went on to explore much of Africa and translate a number of risqué works, including *The Kama Sutra*, *Arabian Nights*, *The Perfumed Garden* and others. He once said he was proud to have committed every sin in the Ten Commandments.

 The first feast day of the carpenter Joseph, husband of Mary.

20 MARCH

In 1981, Britain reintroduces the £50 note, previously withdrawn in 1943 after it was discovered no shopkeeper could ever make change from it. It is still the largest note in British currency. The largest US note in current circulation is $100, though they have produced $10,000-dollar notes in the past. Contrary to myth, neither America nor Britain have ever produced a million-dollar or million-pound note.

Cuthbert, Herbert, Martin of Braga.

21 MARCH

This day is the Vernal Equinox, though it sometimes falls on 20 March. The earth is tilted in respect to its path around the sun. As a result of the tilt, there are times in the year when the normal hemisphere days are longest – the summer solstice, and shortest – the winter solstice. The halfway points are known as equinoxes – days of equal light and dark. The Vernal equinox is also known as the feast of Ostara, a pagan goddess of fertility. The words East and Easter are derived from her name, as is oestrogen, the female hormone.

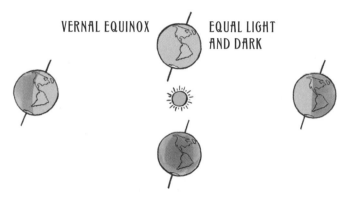

VERNAL EQUINOX   EQUAL LIGHT AND DARK

 Enda, Nicholas von Flue, Serapion of Thmuis.

In 1683 a fire breaks out in Newmarket, causing vast damage. As a result, King Charles II (pictured below) and his brother James (who would later become James II) did not go to the races as they had planned in April. A plot to assassinate them at Rye House in Hertfordshire as they stopped on the journey therefore came to nothing.

In 1769, William Smith, 'The Father of Geology', is born in Oxfordshire. He would go on to produce the first geological map of any country.

On this day in 2001, the Russian space station Mir is moved into a decaying orbit and burns up over the Pacific Ocean near Fiji. The flaming pieces are visible to the naked eye.

 Zacharias.

Gwinear, Toribio of Lima.

24 MARCH

In 1603, Elizabeth I of England and Ireland dies after a reign of 44 years, ending the Elizabethan age that saw the Spanish Armada smashed in 1588, Shakespeare, Sir Francis Drake and Sir Walter Raleigh come to prominence, and a vast period of expansion in English power at sea and on land. Virginia in America is named after this unmarried 'virgin queen'. Interestingly, her mother, Anne Boleyn, had six fingers on one hand. In many paintings of Elizabeth I, the hands are clearly visible – demonstrating that she had not inherited her mother's extra digit. Elizabeth I is buried in Westminster Abbey.

On Elizabeth's death, James I of England (James VI of Scotland) ascends the throne, the first king of Great Britain and Ireland.

 Catherine of Vadstena.

25 MARCH

The Annunciation of Mary the Virgin, or Lady Day, and the feast day of Dismas, the patron saint of condemned prisoners. It is one of the four official 'Quarter Days' in England that divided up the year. As well as being Christian festivals, rent became due on these days, a practice still continued today in some parts.

This day is also Anzac Day, marking the anniversary of the first major military action fought by Australia and New Zealand in World War I. Anzac is an acronym for 'Australia and New Zealand Army Corps'. It is also a day of commemoration for the Australians and New Zealanders who died in the two world wars. The ceremony includes the laying of wreaths and the 'Last Post' being sounded. It is the southern-hemisphere equivalent of Remembrance Sunday.

The feast of the Annunciation, or Lady Day, Dismas.

26 MARCH

In 1902, Cecil Rhodes, founder of Rhodesia, modern-day Zimbabwe, dies.

 Ludger, William of Norwich.

27 MARCH

In 1625, Charles I becomes King of Great Britain and Ireland, also claiming the throne of France, though the French ignore him. He believed he had a 'divine right' to rule, his power granted by god. He went on to lose the English Civil War and was finally beheaded, which just goes to show.

John the Egyptian, Rupert of Salzburg.

28 MARCH

In 1930, Constantinople changes its name to Istanbul. The city was originally named for the Roman Emperor Constantine, the capital of the eastern Roman Empire. Constantine converted to Christianity when he saw a vast cross in the sky. His vision may have coincided with a meteor strike reported around the same time, which was large enough to create a mushroom cloud that looked like a cross. Constantine wanted Christian relics of similar stature to St Peter, so had the bones of another apostle, St Andrew, brought to Constantinople. Some of them were later taken by a monk, who was shipwrecked off the coast of Scotland, which is how Scotland has its link to St Andrew.

Alkeda of Middleham, Gontran.

29 MARCH

In 1461, the Battle of Towton takes place, part of the Wars of the Roses between the houses of Lancaster and York, represented by a red and white rose respectively. Towton is a victory for the Yorkists.

Berthold, Jonah, Mark of Arethusa.

30 MARCH

On this day in 1944, the bombing of Nuremburg takes place. Ninety-seven planes and crews from Bomber Command are lost in one night. More airmen are killed in this single attack than in the Battle of Britain.

Osburga.

31 MARCH

In 1727, Isaac Newton dies, aged 84. He is buried in the nave of Westminster Abbey.

DÉCOUVERTE DE LA THÉORIE DE LA GRAVITATION UNIVERSELLE.
CACAO PUR HOLLANDAIS BENSDORP AMSTERDAM (Hollande)

John Climacus.

I wandered lonely as a Cloud

That floats on high o'er Vales and Hills,

When all at once I saw a crowd,

A host of golden daffodils;

Beside the lake, beneath the trees,

Fluttering and dancing in the breeze.

Continuous as the stars that shine

And twinkle on the milky way,

They stretched in never-ending line

Along the margin of a bay:

Ten thousand saw I at a glance,

Tossing their heads in sprightly dance.

The waves beside them danced, but they

Out-did the sparkling waves in glee:-

A poet could not but be gay

In such a jocund company:

I gazed – and gazed – but little thought

What wealth the show to me had brought:

For oft when on my couch I lie

In vacant or in pensive mood,

They flash upon that inward eye

Which is the bliss of solitude,

And then my heart with pleasure fills,

And dances with the Daffodils.

William Wordsworth

SPRING

This season of growth begins on 21 March at the vernal equinox, when night and day are twelve hours long. From now on, night retreats and the days grow longer. Shoots push through the ground and the world shows green again as winter is forgotten. Snowdrops in hedges herald the spring and birds are everywhere, singing as they prepare their nests for new life.

As your grass begins to need cutting, you might consider buying a couple of fruit saplings from a garden centre. They require very little effort to maintain, barring the odd prune and water in the hot months. In a couple of years you could be enjoying Worcester apples, Conference pears and Victoria plums from your own garden. It doesn't have to be an enormous piece of land: our father planted two Worcester and two Cox's Orange Pippin apple trees in a suburban back garden about forty feet square. The trees are small, but produce enormous amounts of fruit. You'll never regret it.

Feasts and festivals of spring include: Mother's Day on the fourth Sunday in Lent; Commonwealth day on the second Monday in March; the Annunciation on 25 March; the world marble championship at Tinsley Green in Sussex, which takes place around Good Friday; Easter itself; April Fools' Day on 1 April; Palm Sunday, commemorating the entry of Christ into Jerusalem; the Queen's birthday on 21 April; St George's Day on 23 April, May Day on 1 May, cheese rolling at Cooper's Hill on 28 May; and Whitsunday, or Whitsun, the seventh Sunday after Easter, which commemorates the disciples receiving the Holy Spirit. On Maundy Thursday during Easter, the Queen gives pensioners a specially minted silver coin for every year she has lived. This traditional ritual has its origins in monarchs washing the feet of the sick on this day. The royal touch was once believed to cure all manner of ills and the ritual demonstrated humility, just as Jesus washed the feet of the disciples.

Lambs born in autumn reach the shops in spring. Lamb is one of the healthiest meats you can possibly buy, as it is not intensively farmed. The true season for new lamb comes in very late spring. In winter, New Zealand lamb is imported, which is also excellent. Jersey Royal new potatoes come into season in March and go very well with lamb.

Spring is an optimistic, romantic time of year, when young men's thoughts are said to turn to love. Although the weather can be completely unpredictable in a temperate climate like that of Britain, spring officially ends at the summer solstice, around 21 June, when summer begins.

APRIL

April comes from the Latin 'aperire' – to open. Flowers, shops and newspapers open across the land. To the Romans the month was known as 'Aprilis', or possibly Aphrilis, after Aphrodite, the goddess of love.

Easter will come either at the end of March or in April. A moveable feast, it occurs on the first Sunday after the Paschal full moon – the full moon that occurs on the vernal equinox or during the 28 days after it. Easter is by far the most important Christian festival, and one ancient tradition has it that the sun dances on Easter Sunday morning. If you stay up till dawn to test this theory, it is also important to remember not to stare directly at it. Eyesight is more important than dancing suns.

You can sow all sorts of flower bulbs in April, like begonias, for example. However, planting things you can actually eat is more impressive. Broad beans are an easy one and can be sown from a mild March to April. You'll need to tie six-foot-long sticks together to support them, and dig in compost after each annual crop. Bamboo works well and you can always keep the sticks to use again. Our father has grown broad beans in the same spot for thirty years by collecting all the year's vegetable peelings in an old water tank in the garden, then using a spade to dig the resultant black mulch into the ground. His other trick is collecting plastic soft-drink bottles and cutting the tops off so they protect the young shoots from slugs and frost while letting sunlight get through. Plant the seeds two inches deep and six apart. You'll cut the beans about 16 weeks after sowing, though it's easiest to take them as they grow and as you need them.

The other good thing about broad beans is that you only need to buy the large seeds once. After that, you simply have to save a dozen for next year. Remove the long stringy bits along the pods with a sharp knife, slice the pods into pieces and boil them for five to seven minutes. They are delicious.

You can also sow seeds for beetroot or carrots from April to around June. Harvest beetroots when they are no larger than a tennis ball. Onions are also a fairly easy crop, though, like potatoes, they need to be planted rather than grown from seeds.

There are few things as satisfying as eating a carrot you've grown yourself, and proudly telling the family that it tastes much better than the 'rubbish you get in the shops'. It probably does, too.

TRADITIONAL CUSTOMS

Grand National
The Grand National steeplechase is held in mid-April at Aintree racecourse. Considered one of the hardest jump races in the world, it has sixteen fences, all of which are jumped twice except for the water jump and 'The Chair'. The Chair is the highest jump of the course at five feet and two inches with a six-foot ditch before it. The horse Red Rum won the race three times in 1973, 1974 and 1977. He is buried at the winning post at Aintree.

Easter Activities
Easter Monday sees the Epping Stag Hunt, attended in Epping Forest by the Lord Mayor, aldermen and the Corporation of London. The tradition goes back to the thirteenth century.

Easter Tuesday. 'Tuppenny Starver' buns are given out to the congregation at a children's service at the church of St Michael-on-the-Mount in Bristol.

Palm Sunday, the sixth Sunday in Lent. In Herefordshire, 'Pax cakes' or biscuits are handed out to the congregations in Sellack, King's Caple and Hentland. The origins of the custom are not known for certain, but may have come from a bequest, providing for a feast to promote peace and friendship.

On 4 April, at Avenham Park in Preston, the Easter custom of egg-rolling takes place.

1 April, All Fools' Day

In England, the first day of April is known as April Fools' Day; in some northern districts as 'April Noddy Day' and in Scotland and the borders it is 'Huntigowk' Day or 'Gowkin' Day. On this cheerful anniversary, any person may be made to look a fool between the hours of midnight and noon.

There are many traditions of practical jokes on this day: the false summons to the door or the telephone, the empty eggshell upside-down in a cup at breakfast, or a sleeve or trouser-leg sewn up. One favourite is sending a young apprentice to buy 'pigeons' milk', 'elbow grease' or striped paint. In schools today, children are still sent to the music room for 'a long stand', which involves them waiting for ages.

In Scotland, a 'gowk' is a cuckoo, but also means a fool. Victims might be sent about the town with an unread note which says: 'Hunt the gowk another mile', and when read the messenger is sent off again to another house only to be told to go on again. At the stroke of noon all jokes must end. If any attempts are made past midday the intended victim can reply:

April Fool's gone past,
You're the biggest fool at last.

   or

April Noddy's past and gone,
You're the fool and I am none.

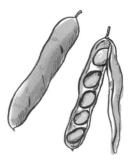

The origin of these customs remains obscure. The fact that they are close to the vernal equinox suggests they are linked to Roman religious festivals like Saturnalia or the medieval feast of fools, where open mockery of respected persons and institutions was allowed. In all ages, men have loved to make fun and deride their fellows and their superiors, and it is the yearly celebration of that dissenting spirit that has kept the fooleries of 1 April alive.

Candle Auctions

At Aldermaston in Berkshire every third year, a piece of land belonging to a local church is auctioned for a given period by the burning of a candle. A pin is put into the candle an inch below the flame and the bidding for the land goes on until it falls out. The last man to make a bid before it falls gets to lease the land for the next three years.

At Tatworth in Somerset a similar auction takes place every year on Old Lady's Day, which is the first Tuesday after 6 April. A piece of land called Stowell Mead is auctioned off in a similar way and the last bid made before the candle burns out secures the Mead for the year. Some of these candle festivals date from the fifteenth century.

Classic Races
In late April, early May, the One Thousand Guineas and Two Thousand Guineas are run at Newmarket, two of the five English Classic races. Like the other three Classics (Oaks Stakes, Epsom Derby Stakes, St. Leger Stakes), the races are for three-year-olds on the flat.

1 APRIL

April Fools' Day.

In the thirteenth century, the King of France presented Henry III with three lions for his menagerie kept at the Tower of London – a gift which became part of the royal coat of arms. The image of three lions can still be seen on English sporting jerseys today. The King's collection of exotic animals was a subject for mockery amongst the courtiers. On the first day of April, the King invited his court to witness the lions washing and bathing in the Tower moat. When they arrived that morning, there were no lions to be seen. This rather weak joke may well be the true origin of April Fools' Day humour.

On this day in 1918, the RAF is founded, combining the Royal Flying Corps and the Royal Naval Air Service.

 Hugh of Grenoble.

2 APRIL

In 1982, the Argentinian head of government, General Galtieri, orders the invasion of the British Falkland Islands, triggering the Falklands War. As they land, a local radio presenter is live on air. He does not want to announce it live and instead plays 'Strangers in the Night' repeatedly until residents understand. The Argentinians insist on referring to the islands as 'The Malvinas', which makes diplomacy difficult as no one can find them on the map.

Also on this day, Nelson wins the battle of Copenhagen in 1801, one of four actions commemorated on his column.

 Francis of Paola, Mary of Egypt.

3 APRIL

In 1882, the outlaw Jesse James is shot dead at the age of 35 by a member of his own gang.

Agape, Irene, Pancras of Taormina, Richard of Chichester.

4 APRIL

In 1581, Queen Elizabeth I knights Francis Drake on the deck of his ship, the *Golden Hind*, after a successful circumnavigation of the globe. By a complete coincidence, he had also brought home vast revenues for the Crown.

Benedict the Black, Isidore of Seville.

5 APRIL

In 1827, Joseph Lister, the 'Father of anti-septic surgery', is born in Upton, Essex. His work, in conjunction with that of Louis Pasteur and the Hungarian doctor Ignaz Semmelweis, lowers death rates after surgery dramatically in British hospitals. Lister found that spraying a constant mist of carbolic acid over a wound and his own hands prevented sepsis. The drawback was that the skin of his hands became inflamed by constant exposure to the acid.

 Vincent Ferrer.

6 APRIL

In 1896, the first modern Olympic games is held in Athens. A Greek, Spyridon Louis, wins the marathon. An Irishman, John Boland, is on holiday in Greece at the time and enters the men's tennis competition. To his surprise, he wins the gold medal.

William of Aebelholt.

7 APRIL

In 1739, highwayman Dick Turpin is hanged in York.

 John-Baptist de La Salle, Nilus of Sora.

8 APRIL

In 1838, Brunel's ship, the SS *Great Western*, sets off from Bristol, racing the SS *Sirius* to New York. The *Sirius* had set off from Ireland four days before and reached New York only one day ahead of the *Great Western*. Brunel's ship reaches a top speed of 8.66 knots and is later awarded the Blue Riband for setting a transatlantic record.

 Perpetuus.

9 APRIL

In 1413, Henry V is crowned at Westminster Abbey, the ablest of the English medieval warrior kings. He will go on to win the battle of Agincourt, re-conquer Normandy, of which he was Duke, and marry the daughter of the King of France, becoming regent of that country.

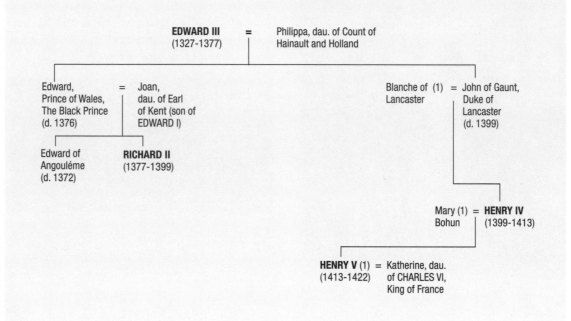

Waudru, the patroness of Mons in Belgium, where she built a convent.

10 APRIL

In 1912, the White Star Line passenger ship RMS *Titanic* leaves from Southampton Docks on her maiden voyage to America. 'RMS' stands for 'Royal Mail Steamer', as she carried the mail as well as passengers. The ship is also known as the SS *Titanic*, SS standing for 'Steam Ship'.

Beocca and Hethor, Hedda of Peterborough.

In 1957, Britain agrees to give Singapore self-rule.

 Gemma Galgani, Stanislas of Crakow.

In 1961, the cosmonaut Yuri Gagarin becomes the first man in space, orbiting the earth for 108 minutes and travelling at 17,000 miles an hour, so that he also became the fastest man alive.

Sabas the Goth, Teresa of the Andes, Zeno of Verona.

13 APRIL

In 1892, Sir Arthur Harris is born, later known as 'Bomber' Harris for coordinating Bomber Command during World War II.

 Carpus, Martin I and Papylus.

14 APRIL

In 1970, the *Apollo 13* Lunar expedition is crippled by an explosion on board, resulting in the famous, oft-misquoted message: 'Houston, we've had a problem.'

Tiburtius, buried with St Valerian and St. Maximus on the Via Appia near Rome.

15 APRIL

In 1452, Leonardo da Vinci is born in Tuscany, Italy.

On this day in 1912, after being struck by an iceberg close to midnight on the fourteenth, RMS *Titanic* sinks on her maiden voyage, with the loss of more than 1,500 lives.

 Paternus of Wales, Ruadhan.

16 APRIL

In 1746, the Battle of Culloden takes place, the final clash between the Jacobites and Hanoverians in the second Jacobite Rebellion of 1745. The Jacobites support the right of Charles Stewart, better known as Bonny Prince Charlie, to the throne of England and Scotland. They are defeated and George II remains in power.

FRANKLYN'S CIGARETTES.

BATTLE OF CULLODEN.

Benedict Joseph Labre, Fructuosus of Braga, Magnus of Orkney. Most famously, this day is the feast of St. Bernadette, a frail asthmatic who made Lourdes a place of pilgrimage for millions after seeing visions of Mary there.

17 APRIL

In 1961, the Bay of Pigs invasion of Cuba takes place. American-organised Cuban exiles attempt to overthrow Fidel Castro, but fail.

 Donnan, Robert of Chaise-Dieu, Stephen Harding.

18 APRIL

In 1955, Albert Einstein dies. His last words are unknown as he speaks in German and the nurse does not understand that language.

Laserian, Apollonius.

19 APRIL

In 1770, Captain Cook discovers Australia, to the enormous surprise of the Aborigines.

On this day in 1824, the poet Lord Byron dies at Missolonghi in Greece, after taking command of a Greek brigade, aiding them in their struggle for independence from the Turks.

 Alphege, Pope Leo IX.

20 APRIL

In 1657, the Battle of Santa Cruz takes place in the Canary Islands, the greatest victory over the Spanish since the Armada in 1588. Sixteen Spanish ships are destroyed by an English fleet commanded by Admiral Blake.

Agnes of Montepulciano.

21 APRIL

This day in 753 BC is the traditional date for the founding of Rome by twin brothers named Romulus and Remus. Romulus would later murder Remus.

On this day in 1509, Henry VIII becomes King of England.

Also on this day in 1926, Queen Elizabeth II is born in London.

 Simeon Barsabba'e. It is also the feast day of St. Anselm, a great philosopher and theologian of the eleventh century.

22 APRIL

In 1833, Richard Trevithick dies, inventor of the world's first steam locomotive.

On this day in 1951, the Battle of Imjin River is fought in the Korean War. Two Victoria Crosses are awarded for this single action, to Lieutenant Colonel Carne and Lieutenant Curtis.

 Conrad of Parzham, Theodore of Sykeon.

23 APRIL

St George's Day. Believed to be Shakespeare's birthday in 1564. Interestingly, Shakespeare also died on this day of a 'surfeit of alcohol' in 1616, after celebrating his birthday with Ben Jonson and other writers and actors. He is buried in Stratford-upon-Avon.

J. M. W. Turner, perhaps Britain's greatest painter, shares this date of birth, born in Covent Garden, London, in 1775. He died in Chiswick in 1851 and is buried in St Paul's Cathedral.

Finally, on this day in 1983, pound coins were issued by the Royal Mint for the first time.

 Adalbert of Prague.

103

24 APRIL

In 1953 Winston Churchill is knighted by Queen Elizabeth II. He wins the Nobel Prize for Literature in the same year, 'for his mastery of historical and biographical description as well as for brilliant oratory in defending exalted human values.'

 Egbert, Euphrasia Pelletier, Mellitus.

25 APRIL

In 1599, Oliver Cromwell is born. He goes on to become Lord Protector of the English Commonwealth and resides at Hampton Court after overseeing the execution of Charles I.

 William of Monte Vergine. It is also the feast day of St. Mark, gospel writer and disciple. His bones lie in Venice at the Basilica San Marco.

In 1607, Captain John Smith lands with colonists in Virginia (named for the Virgin Queen, Elizabeth I), establishing the first permanent settlement.

 Cletus, Stephen of Perm.

In 1992, Betty Boothroyd becomes the first woman Speaker in the House of Commons.

Maughold, Toribio of Lima, Zita.

28 APRIL

In 1876, Prime Minister Disraeli makes Queen Victoria Empress of India. Her reign is the longest of any British monarch, stretching from 1837 to 1901.

On this day in 1945, Mussolini is executed by Italian resistance fighters. He is shot repeatedly. His body is publicly displayed and then shot again, just to make absolutely certain.

Finally, on this day in 2001, billionaire Dennis Tito becomes the first space tourist, with a trip to the International Space Station. The Americans only allow the flight when he promises to pay for anything he breaks.

 Louis Grignion, Paul of the Cross.

29 APRIL

In 1945, American forces liberate the concentration camp of Dachau. The soldiers are so appalled at what they see that they execute the commandant and five hundred of his troops.

 Catherine of Siena, Hugh of Cluny, Robert of Molesme.

30 APRIL

In 1975, the war in Vietnam ends as Saigon surrenders to the Viet Cong.

Erconwald, Joseph of Cottolengo, Marian and James, who were third century martyrs and died together.

MAY

To the Romans, the month was 'Maius', named after Maia, the goddess of growth. The Romans also celebrated the feast of Flora in this month, another goddess of fruits and flowers. Not too unexpectedly, they danced and sang in the fields, though not with whips this time, as they did in February. That feast became May Day, celebrated primarily in England. Generally, it involves dancing around a Maypole on the first day of the month. There might even be Morris dancing, which usually involves six or eight men with sticks facing each other and beating out a fast rhythm. Beer is a vital part of this event.

In addition, young girls can wash their faces in the early-morning dew, which makes them beautiful for the year. In the seventeenth century, the poet Herrick wrote:

'There's not a budding boy or girl, this day,
But is got up, and gone to bring in May.'

In some villages today, such as Ickwell in Bedfordshire, a 'Queen of the May' is still crowned – a human personification of the goddess Flora. It is a welcome to summer and an innocent celebration to banish the dark months. There will always be some who see a hidden meaning in such things, but sometimes a Maypole is just a stick.

The Anglo-Saxons called the month 'thrimilce', as cows could be milked three times a day. They were clearly a dour lot and missed the whole point.

One well-known old rhyme for May goes as follows: 'Cast ne'er a clout till May is out' – meaning don't remove your winter clothing until the summer has arrived in earnest. Good advice.

THE MAY-POLE

ILLUSTRATED BY

G·A·KON·
STAM·
E·CAS·
ELLA·
AND
N·CAS·
ELLA·

THOS. DE LA RUE & CO. LONDON.

TRADITIONAL CUSTOMS

In High Wycombe, Buckinghamshire, the local mayor is weighed in May. A year later, they are weighed again. If he has gained weight, the macebearer says 'and some more!' and the crowd jeers cheerfully. If he has not gained weight, the cry is 'and no more!', which brings cheering and applause.

May Bank Holiday

The Spring Bank Holiday Monday in May sees the annual cheese-rolling event at Cooper's Hill in Gloucester. A rolling circular cheese is chased down a steep hill by young men at high speed. The first one down claims the cheese.

On that same Bank Holiday, Morris dancing takes place at Bampton in Oxfordshire.

In mid-May in Durham, the newly elected mayor throws a handful of 5p coins to the crowd as he or she comes out. On the third Thursday in May, the mayor at Harwich in Essex throws buns from the window of the council chamber instead.

Around Ascension Day in May, various customs persist that have to do with 'beating the bounds' or blessing the boundaries of parishes. Such events go on at the Tower of London, the parishes of St Michael in the Northgate and St Mary the Virgin in Oxford, and many others.

29 May, Garland Day, Castleton, Derbyshire
This involves a procession through the town of a 'King' and 'Queen' on horses. The King is draped in a bell of flowers so large that he can hardly be seen. He is accompanied by Morris dancers and his 'Queen'. The exact origins are unknown, though it is obviously of a piece with May celebrations generally.

Motorcycle TT Race
The Isle of Man Motorcycle TT Race practices begin on 27 May, with the races being run up to 9 June.

1 MAY

The ancient pagan feast day of Beltane, which celebrates the spring. In ancient Rome it was the Festival of Fools, where society's rules could be broken without punishment. In Britain, it is also known as Gosling Day, or Horse Ribbon Day.

On this day in 1707, the Act of Union comes into effect, joining England, Wales and Scotland. The first article of the act describes the Union flag as a combination of the cross of St Andrew and the cross of St George. The final design will also incorporate the cross of St Patrick of Ireland. British ships fly the flag on the jackstaff, which is why it is often called the 'Union Jack'. On land, it is correctly called the 'Union Flag'.

Also on this day in 1999, the body of George Leigh Mallory is found near the summit of Everest, having been missing since an expedition in 1924. It is not known whether he died on the way up or whether he and his climbing partner Andrew Irving were actually successful long before Edmund Hilary and Tenzing Norgay in 1953.

Peregrine Laziosi, Ultan. This day is also the feast of Joseph the Workman, husband to the Virgin Mary.

2 MAY

In 1982, Argentina's only cruiser, the *General Belgrano*, is sunk by two Tigerfish torpedoes from HMS *Conqueror*.

    On this day in 1947, James Dyson is born. As inventor of the Dual Cyclone bagless vacuum cleaner, he will go on to become a billionaire. It took four and a half *thousand* prototypes to arrive at one good enough to sell. For that level of determination alone, he deserves his place here.

 Athanasius, Mafalda.

3 MAY

In 1947, a new Japanese Constitution comes into effect, having been written the previous year. It was drawn up by the staff of General Douglas MacArthur, who had accepted the Japanese surrender. The constitution removed the power of the emperor, gave the vote to all and established a bill of rights. It also prohibited a standing army.

 Philip, one of the twelve apostles. Theodosius of the Caves. This is also the feast day of James the Lesser. Although he too was an apostle, he is known as James the Lesser to distinguish him from James, brother to John, two more of the apostles or disciples of Jesus.

4 MAY

In 1904, Charles Rolls and engineer Henry Royce meet and agree to form a partnership. Charles Rolls sold cars in London, then a prestigious occupation. In July 1906 they produce the 'Silver Ghost' Rolls-Royce. Later on, Rolls meets the Wright brothers and becomes passionate about flight. He is killed when his Wright flyer crashes in 1910.

On this day in 1979, Britain elects Margaret Thatcher, the first woman to be Prime Minister. She serves three consecutive terms.

 Florian, Gothard, Pelagia of Tarsus.

5 MAY

In 1821, Napoleon dies on the island of St Helena.

On this day in 1961, Alan Shepard becomes the first American in space in the 'Freedom 7' mission flight into orbit, part of the Mercury series of flights that will be followed by the famous Gemini and Apollo missions. He reaches space only a month behind Yuri Gagarin

Also on this day in 1980, the SAS assault the Iranian embassy to save 26 hostages from six terrorists protesting at the rule of the Ayatollah Khomeini. The SAS rescue all 26 in eleven minutes, killing five of the terrorists and capturing the sixth

 Hilary of Arles, Jutta.

6 MAY

In 1840, the 'Penny Black', the world's first stamp, is issued.

On this day in 1910, Edward VII dies, ending the decade-long 'Edwardian Period'.

Also on this day in 1937, the Hindenburg airship is destroyed. Finally, in 1954, Roger Bannister breaks the four-minute mile for the first time.

 Edbert, Marian and James.

7 MAY

In 1910, George V becomes king.

On this day in 1915, the SS *Lusitania* is sunk by a German submarine off the coast of Ireland, killing 1,200 men, women and children.

John of Beverley, Lindhard.

8 MAY

VE day, 1945: Victory in Europe, as German forces finally surrender after six years of the bloodiest war in history. Allied countries including Britain, Canada, Australia, New Zealand, America and Russia lost more than sixty million men, women and children in the conflict.

 Peter of Tarantaise, Victor.

9 MAY

In 1671, the attempted theft of the crown jewels by the Irishman Colonel Thomas Blood takes place. One of history's most likeable rogues, Blood had fought against Charles I in the Civil War, and had to flee England when Charles II was restored to the throne. His plan to steal the jewels involved him disguising himself as a parson and knocking the Keeper of the Jewels on the head with a mallet. Blood then discovered that the king's sceptre would not fit in his bag. His companion was in the process of sawing it in half when the Keeper of the Jewels came round and summoned help. Astonishingly, King Charles II so enjoyed the man's wit and charm that Blood was not only pardoned, but also given lands in Ireland. Alternatively, Blood managed to blackmail Charles II with something he revealed only to the king in private. We'll never know for certain.

 Pachomius.

10 MAY

In 1940, Neville Chamberlain resigns as head of the government, having failed to preserve 'Peace for our time'. Churchill becomes Prime Minister, saying 'I have nothing to offer but blood, toil, tears and sweat.'

Antonino, Isidore the Farm-servant.

11 MAY

In 1812, Prime Minister Spencer Perceval is assassinated. Unlike American Presidents, he is the only British Prime Minister to date to be killed in this way. Perceval's assassin, John Bellingham, is later hanged.

Asaph, Comgall, Francis di Girolamo.

In 1809, the Battle of Oporto takes place during the Peninsular War in Portugal. An Anglo–Portuguese force under Wellington defeats the army of Marshal Soult, capturing 1,500 and killing 600 for a loss of only 120 men. As a result, Napoleon's armies are forced to retreat from Portugal. On the night of the twelfth, Wellington sits in the French headquarters and eats the meal that had been prepared for Soult.

In 1981, Pope John Paul II survives an assassination attempt by a Turkish Moslem. In those days, before the modern rash of Islamic terrorism, other motives were suspected. The shooter, Mehmet Agcar, is pardoned by Italy in 2000, then returned to Turkey to serve another ten-year sentence for killing a liberal newspaper editor in 1979.

 Andrew Fournet, Euthymius the Enlightened.

Epiphanius of Salamis, Germanus of Constantinople, Ignatius of Laconi. St. Pancras, after whom the London station is named, also has his feast day here.

14 MAY

In 1948, the State of Israel is declared, sanctioned by the United Nations. The following day, the British mandate in Palestine expires and the armies of Egypt, Syria, Jordan, Iraq and Lebanon all attack at the same time. Israel fights them all and forces each country to accept an armistice in 1949. Hostilities continue throughout the twentieth century, with outbreaks such as the 1956 Suez Crisis, where Israel fought with Britain and France against Egypt, and the 'Six Day War' in 1967, when Israel was again attacked by Egypt, Jordan, Iraq and Syria. Despite almost constant conflict with Arab nations, Israel has survived for the last sixty years. The region remains in crisis into the twenty-first century.

···· 1949 Armistice Line

▨ 1949 Jordanian controlled

▨ 1949 Egyptian controlled

▥ 1967 Israeli occupied lands

Mary Mazzarello, Michael Garicoïts. It is also the feast day of the Apostle Matthias, who was chosen by the others to replace Judas after his suicide.

15 MAY

In 1957, Britain conducts her first atomic-bomb tests on Christmas Island in the Pacific, exploding three of them at 18,000 feet. The operation is code-named 'Grapple'.

 Dympna, Hallvard.

16 MAY

In 2001, John Prescott, the Deputy Prime Minister, punches protestor Craig Evans after Evans threw an egg at him in Rhyl, north Wales. The girlfriend of Evans said, 'Craig threw an egg at Mr Prescott, who was walking past after getting off the battle bus. Then Mr Prescott grabbed him by the scruff of the neck and thumped him.'

It wasn't a particularly good left jab, it has to be said, but Prescott was hampered by the press of the crowd.

 Brendan the Voyager, Honorius of Amiens, Simon Stock, Ubaldo, John of Nepomuk.

17 MAY

In 1900, the Siege of Mafeking in South Africa is lifted. Among those who have held out against Dutch forces for 217 days is Robert Baden-Powell. It was he who organised much of the defence. He is promoted to Major General and made a knight. It is said that his idea for the Scout movement came from a cadet corps of boys who were part of the defence force at Mafeking.

Also on this day in 1943, the Dam Busters crews arrive just after midnight at the dams on the river Ruhr in Germany. The bouncing bombs they use were invented for the purpose by Barnes Wallis, who also designed the Wellington Bomber. The Mohne and Eder Dam are breached, but the Sorpe Dam held.

 Paschal Baylon.

18 MAY

In 1588, the Spanish Armada sets sail from Spain. (Some sources give the date as 29 May.) They reach England in July of that year. They would have set off earlier, but Sir Francis Drake had led a small fleet to Cadiz, destroying 31 ships and capturing 6 intact. Drake later referred to this as 'singeing the King of Spain's beard', an action that put back the Spanish preparations for war by a year. Famously, Drake is playing bowls in Plymouth when the Armada is sighted. He insists on finishing his game before going to his ship. It is true that great storms smashed the Spanish fleet, but they came after the sea battle, where they were soundly beaten and forced to flee.

Also on this day, in 1991, the first Briton – Helen Sharman – reaches space, launching on this day with the soviet craft *Soyuz TM-12* from Kazakhstan. Astonishingly, she answered an advert that said 'Astronaut wanted. No experience necessary', and was selected from more than 13,000 applicants. Technically, she is a cosmonaut as it was a Russian operation. Sharman took a photograph of the queen with her as well as a passport in case she landed outside Russia.

 Eric, Felix of Cantalice, Pope John I.

19 MAY

In 1536, the execution of Anne Boleyn takes place, Henry VIII's second wife and mother to Elizabeth I. She stood accused of adultery with several men, including her husband's tennis coach and her own brother George, which doesn't seem very likely. A French executioner was brought from Calais. A swordsman, it was thought that he might do a cleaner job than an axe-man, who sometimes took two or three blows to remove a head. When Anne heard this, she said, 'He shall not have much trouble, for I have a little neck.' When the time came, it took a single blow, and she is buried in a chapel at the Tower of London.

Pope Celestine V, Dunstan, Yves.

20 MAY

In 1806, John Stuart Mill, one of the great thinkers of the nineteenth century, is born. His essays and books, particularly *On Liberty*, are vital reading even today.

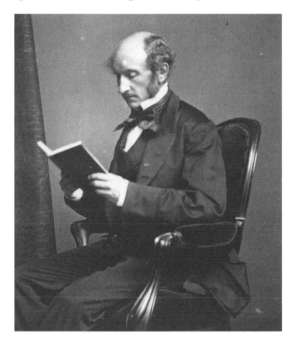

Bernadine of Siena, Ethelbert of the East Angles.

21 MAY

In 1840, Captain William Hobson declares British sovereignty over the whole of New Zealand. When a French frigate for the Nanto-Bordelaise trading company arrives two months later, they are too late. Hobson will later become New Zealand's first governor.

Godric.

In 1455, the Battle of St Albans takes place, the first major battle of the War of the Roses between the houses of Lancaster and York. The war finally ends with the Battle of Bosworth Field in 1485, where Richard III is killed. Victory went to the Lancastrian Henry Tudor, who takes the throne as Henry VII.

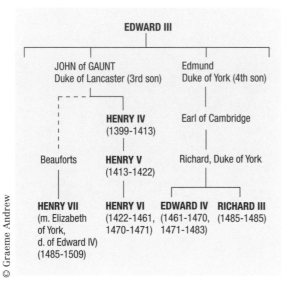

© Graeme Andrew

EDWARD III

JOHN of GAUNT
Duke of Lancaster (3rd son)

Edmund
Duke of York (4th son)

HENRY IV
(1399-1413)

Earl of Cambridge

Beauforts

HENRY V
(1413-1422)

Richard, Duke of York

HENRY VII
(m. Elizabeth
of York,
d. of Edward IV)
(1485-1509)

HENRY VI
(1422-1461,
1470-1471)

EDWARD IV
(1461-1470,
1471-1483)

RICHARD III
(1485-1485)

 Rita of Cascia.

In 1701, Captain William Kidd is hanged for piracy and murder in London, having made the mistake of preying on English vessels. He was originally employed by the crown to hunt pirates, but went to the bad himself in 1697.

Euphrosyne of Polotsk, Ivo of Chartres, Willliam of Rochester.

24 MAY

In 1683, the world's first public museum opens – the Ashmolean Museum in Oxford. The exhibits include a stuffed dodo, which no one realises is the only preserved dodo in existence. At a later period, during a museum clear-out, the somewhat tatty bird is dumped on a fire. It is rescued by a curator, but only a few bits survive.

On this day in 1941, the pride of the British Navy, the Hood, is destroyed by the German battleship *Bismarck*, just after six in the morning. The nation is in shock. Churchill gives the order: 'Sink the *Bismarck*!'

During the period of the British Empire (a noble period of unlimited good things), this was Empire Day.

David of Scotland, Simeon the Stylite (Younger).

In 1659, Richard Cromwell, son of Oliver, resigns as Lord Protector, leading the way to the Restoration of the Monarchy and the reign of Charles II.

This day is also the feast day of the Venerable Bede, known as 'The Father of English History' for his work *The Ecclesiastical History of the English Nation*, written in the early eighth century. He was the first writer in English prose and is the only Englishman mentioned by Dante in his *Paradiso*.

Aldhelm, Mary Magdelen dei Pazzi. The Three Marys – Mary Magdelen, Mary the wife of Cleophas (mentioned in the Gospel of John) and Mary the mother of James.

In 1798, income tax is introduced in Britain for the first time, as a 'temporary measure' to raise funds to fight the French in the Napoleonic wars. The Prime Minister, William Pitt, admits that the idea is 'repugnant to the customs and manners of the nation' but goes ahead regardless. The crisis with France passed and the law was repealed in 1816. Unfortunately, it raised so much money for the government that they were unlikely to forget such a good wheeze, reintroducing income tax in 1842.

Mariana of Quito, Philip Neri.

27 MAY

In 1941, the battleship *Bismarck* is crippled by Swordfish torpedo planes, severing the link to the rudder. Out of control, the *Bismarck* heads straight for the British fleet, under Admiral Tovey. Capital ships including the *Rodney*, *King George V* and the *Dorsetshire* hammer the *Bismarck*, until a ceasefire is ordered at 10.15 a.m. The German crew then abandon ship, scuttling *Bismarck* as they go. The most powerful battleship in the Atlantic is destroyed at last.

Julius of Durostorum. Also the feast day of St. Augustine of Canterbury who was sent by Pope Gregory I to convert the English to Christianity. He arrived in Kent in 597 AD.

28 MAY

In 1982, the Battle of Goose Green takes place during the Falklands War. Despite being out-numbered two-to-one, the British forces are successful in routing the Argentineans after fierce hand-to-hand fighting. Lieutenant Colonel H. Jones is posthumously awarded the Victoria Cross. In addition, twenty other military decorations are awarded for gallant service and heroism.

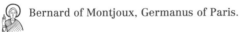 Bernard of Montjoux, Germanus of Paris.

29 MAY

Oak-Apple, Royal Oak or Acorn Day, commemorating the time Charles II had to hide in an oak tree to escape his enemies.

Also on this day, in 1953, Edmund Hilary and Tenzing Norgay reach the summit of Everest. Interestingly, Everest is not the biggest mountain on earth if you take the height from top to bottom. The actual highest mountain is Hawaii, though, to be fair, most of it is underwater, which hampers even serious climbers.

 Bona of Pisa.

30 MAY

The feast day of Joan of Arc, the patron saint of France. She fought the English, was burned at the stake and had her ashes thrown into the Seine by the English so no relics could be taken. She died in 1431.

 Ferdinand III of Castille, Joan of Arc.

31 MAY

In 1859, the bell of the Great Clock at Westminster, popularly known as 'Big Ben', rings for the first time across London. The bell was cast in Whitechapel and transported to its new home by teams of horses.

 Petronilla.

JUNE

To the Romans, the month would have been 'Junius' and associated with Juno, queen of the gods and long-suffering wife to Jupiter, who was forever nipping off with young maidens before turning them into swans and suchlike. She was the mother to Mars in their pantheon. To the Greeks, she was known as Hera, wife to Zeus and mother to Ares.

Father's Day comes on the third Sunday of this month, begun originally in 1909 by Sonora Dodd of Washington.

The summer solstice is 21 June (though it does occasionally fall on 20 June). It is the longest day of the year, when the northern hemisphere is pointing towards the sun. Up to 20,000 people gravitate to Stonehenge in Wiltshire on this day to watch the dawn. Depending on the number of police present, it is no longer possible to touch the stones.

Midsummer's Day is of course a pagan festival, associated with druids and divination – telling the future. Up to the sixteenth century, bonfires were lit all over the country, both as a symbol of peace and brotherhood and also to cleanse the air of sickness. One or two summer fires still linger on in modern times, such as the Whalton Baal Fire in Northumberland on 4 July. One old legend has it that if you watch a church porch on Midsummer's Eve at midnight, you'll see the image of anyone in the parish who will die in the coming year. It was also meant to be possible for a young girl to see the name of her future husband by tossing hemp

seeds over her shoulder. Unless the girl in question can read Braille, this does not seem likely to work, however. Goodwood Festival of Speed is held from 22 to 24 June at Goodwood House in Sussex.

For the Anglo-Saxons, June was known as 'Sēromōnath' – the 'dry month'.

TRADITIONAL CUSTOMS

Appleby Horse Fair

The Appleby Horse Fair takes place in the first week of June, at Appleby in West-moreland. It is a traditional gypsy gathering, though all are welcome. As well as racing, stalls and all horse-related activities, the horses are taken into the river Eden for a wash and a swim.

Classic Races

The third English Classic is The Oaks, which is run in early June at Epsom. It is for fillies only and began in 1779. The fourth Classic, the Epsom Derby, is run at Epsom later in June and began in 1780. Both are on the flat. Interestingly, it is called the Derby after the Earl of Derby. He and Sir Charles Bunbury tossed a coin to decide the name of the race. If the Earl had lost, it would be called the Epsom Bunbury. It was at the Epsom Derby that suffragette Emily Davidson was killed when she stepped in front of King George V's horse, Anmer, in 1913.

Knaresborough Bed Race

Around 9 June, the Knaresborough Bed Race takes place in North Yorkshire. This involves around fifty themed and decorated beds each pushed by a team, though someone must always be in the bed. The course is gruelling and involves crossing a deep river at one point.

The Duke of Edinburgh's birthday is on 10 June. Gun salutes are fired in Hyde Park and at the Tower of London.

Royal Ascot

Royal Ascot takes place near Windsor from 19–23 June, with Ladies' Day on 21 June. It was begun by Queen Anne in 1711, when she purchased land for the course. The Queen Anne Stakes is the first race at Royal Ascot each year.

Bawming the Thorn

On or around 29 June, children in Appleton, Cheshire, 'Bawm the Thorn', which involves decorating and dancing around a hawthorn tree in the village. The original Appleton thorn is said to have been taken from a cutting of the Glastonbury thorn, itself once the staff of Joseph of Arimathea, which took root as he arrived in England.

Wimbledon

On the last week in June and the first week of July, the Wimbledon Tennis Championship is staged by the All England Lawn Tennis and Croquet Club in London, a competition that goes back to 1877. The first Wimbledon champion was Spencer Gore. A ladies' tournament began in 1884, the first of which was won by Maud Watson.

The Ashes

The Ashes series of Test matches between England and Australia is played every two years, with each country taking it in turns to host. As it is a summer game, that can mean the Ashes are between 18 and 30 months apart. In England, they begin in June and go right through to September.

1 JUNE

On this day in 1794, the channel fleet under Lord Howe gains a famous victory over a French fleet under Villaret de Joyeuse. Six French ships are captured and one sunk. After that, the French Admiral isn't particularly 'joyeuse' at all. In Britain, the day is still sometimes called 'The Glorious First of June' in memory of the battle.

Also on this day, in 1907, Frank Whittle, the inventor of the jet engine, is born in Coventry. He lives until 1996, seeing his invention used all over the world. He is commemorated in the RAF chapel in Westminster Abbey.

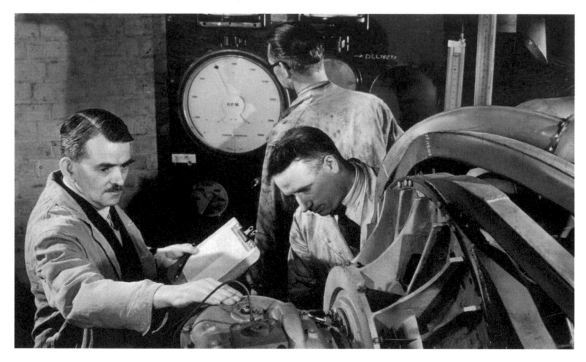

Justin, Pamphilus.

2 JUNE

The feast day of Erasmus, sometimes known as St Elmo – the patron saint of sailors.

On this day in 1953, Queen Elizabeth II is crowned in Westminster Abbey. Daughter to George VI and the great, great granddaughter of Queen Victoria, she has a direct royal line back to William the Conqueror.

Erasmus, The Martyrs of Lyons, Marcellinus and Peter, who were fourth century martyrs. Also, Nicephorus of Constantinople.

3 JUNE

In 1865, George V, son of Edward VII and grandson of Queen Victoria, is born. He is the second Emperor of India and rules the British Empire during World War I. Not a great patron of the arts, he said his favourite opera was *La Boheme*, as it was the shortest. He is buried in St George's Chapel, Windsor.

Clotilde, Kevin, martyrs of Uganda.

4 JUNE

In 1738, George III is born. He was the first of the Hanoverian line to actually be born in England, at Norfolk House, London. He is also the first to speak fluent English. Due to his love of agriculture, he was popularly known as 'Farmer George'.

GEORGE I (1714-1727)	=	Sophia Dorothea, dau. of Duke of Brunswick and Celle (div. (under Hanoverian Law) 1692)
GEORGE II (1727-1760)	=	Caroline, dau. of Margrave of Brandenburg-Anspach
Augusta of Saxe-Gotha-Altenberg	=	Frederick Lewis, Prince of Wales (d. 1751)
GEORGE III (1760-1820)	=	Sophia Charlotte of Mecklenburg-Strelitz

© Graeme Andrew

Francis Caracciolo, Petroc.

5 JUNE

In 1963, Minister John Profumo resigns, after finally admitting a liaison with call-girl Christine Keeler. He then worked for over forty years at Toynbee Hall, a charity for the elderly in Whitechapel. For this work, he was awarded a CBE (Commander of the British Empire).

Boniface of Crediton.

6 JUNE

In 1862, the poet Henry Newbolt is born in Staffordshire. He is best known for the wonderful poem 'Vitai Lampada', which begins, 'There's a breathless hush in the close tonight...'

> There's a breathless hush on the Close to-night
> Ten to make and the match to win
> A bumping pitch and a blinding light,
> An hour to play, and the last man in.
> And it's not for the sake of a ribboned coat.
> Or the selfish hope of a season's fame,
> But his captain's hand on his shoulder smote
> 'Play up! Play up! And play the game!'
>
> **Extract from 'Vitai Lampada'**
> **by Newbolt**

Jarlath of Tuam.

7 JUNE

In 1942, the Battle of Midway in the Pacific ends after three days of ferocious fighting. It began on 4 June with Japanese air raids on the US military base on Midway Island, a thousand miles north of Hawaii. The American response involved the Pacific fleet. They sank or damaged ten Japanese destroyers and four aircraft carriers, losing none of their own ships. Admiral Chester Nimitz of the Pacific fleet said of the battle, 'Pearl Harbor has now been partially avenged.'

 Colman of Dromore, Robert of Newminster.

8 JUNE

In 1536, Henry VIII's daughters are declared illegitimate on his order, to allow the children of his latest wife, Jane Seymour, to inherit. Sadly, she dies giving birth to her son, Edward after a caesarean without anaesthetic. Though he survives to be king, Edward VI dies aged only 15, leaving the throne to be contested and then taken by Mary and Elizabeth in turn.

 Meriana the Elder, William of York.

9 JUNE

In 1982, the twenty-pence piece is introduced to British currency.

Columba, Pelagia of Antioch, Primus and Felician.

10 JUNE

In 1921, Prince Philip, Duke of Edinburgh, is born in Corfu. He will later serve in the Royal Navy as midshipman and then lieutenant during World War II. He marries Princess Elizabeth in 1947, six years before her coronation. He is the patron of the Duke of Edinburgh Awards Scheme, which has around quarter of a million young people taking part at any one time. To qualify for the Bronze, Silver and Gold Award, participants must complete tasks in four areas: Expedition, Skills, Physical Recreation and Service.

 Margaret of Scotland, Ithamar.

11 JUNE

In 1509, Henry VIII marries Katherine of Aragon, a Spanish princess who had previously been married to Henry's older brother Arthur until his untimely death. Interestingly, it was the young Henry who was sent to meet Katherine on her first arrival in England from Spain. When no male heir is forthcoming, it is Henry's divorce from Katherine that leads indirectly to the Protestant Reformation in England and war between Catholics and Protestants for generations.

On this night in 1962, Frank Morris and two brothers, Clarence and John Anglin, escape from Alcatraz. Their plan involved creating dummies for their beds, a raft, and inflatable life-vests to help them survive the freezing water between the prison and land. They have never been caught.

Barnabas, who was a friend of St. Paul and named as an Apostle, though he was not one of the twelve.

12 JUNE

In 1897, the Swiss Officer's knife is patented. It becomes a staple of all camping trips and the like, though most people who use one have a story of the blade closing on their fingers and gashing them deeply. The Leatherman multi-tool, with its locking blades and decent sized pliers, is much better for all-round use, though it does lack a corkscrew.

Eskil, John of Sahagun, Pope Leo III.

13 JUNE

In 232 BC, Alexander the Great dies at the age of 33 after a fever. He has never lost a battle. At around the same age, Julius Caesar later weeps at a statue to Alexander in Cadiz and visits his preserved body in Alexandria, Egypt. It has since been lost.

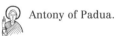 Antony of Padua.

14 JUNE

In 1381, the Peasants Revolt takes place, under Walter 'Wat' Tyler, Jack Straw and John Ball, a renegade priest. The rebellion is widespread in the east of England, with 'The Men of Essex' joining factions from Kent and other places. The uprising is due to a new poll tax. It results in the Tower of London being attacked, the murder of both the Lord Chancellor and the Archbishop of Canterbury and the destruction of the Savoy Palace.

On this day in 1927, Jerome K. Jerome dies. He is the author of *Three Men in a Boat*, a strong contender for the funniest book ever written.

Also on this day in 1982, Argentina surrenders and the Falklands War ends.

 Elisha, Methodius of Constantinople.

15 JUNE

In 1381, the Peasants Revolt is crushed at Smithfield and St John's Fields, London. King Richard II goes back on promises made to the rebels. They are betrayed, captured and tortured, the rebellion is broken and the poll tax levied.

On this date in 1998, the two-pound coin is issued by the Royal Mint.

 Edburga of Winchester, a grand-daughter of King Alfred the Great. Also, Germaine of Pibrac, Vitus.

16 JUNE

In 1963, Valentina Tereshkova becomes the first woman in space on the mission Vostok 6. She makes 48 orbits of the earth and is up there for 71 hours.

Cyricus and Julitta, John Regis, Tikhon of Amathus.

17 JUNE

In 1239, Edward I is born, who ends hopes of Welsh independence by making his son 'Prince of Wales'. Legend has it that he promised the Welsh a ruler who would speak no English – then producing the infant son. Edward I builds huge castles in Wales before moving on to subdue Scotland, led at that time by Robert the Bruce and the famous rebel William Wallace. Edward's final command to his son, Edward II, was to boil the flesh from his bones and carry the bones in every battle against the Scots until they were destroyed. His son goes on to lose the Battle of Bannockburn.

 Botolph, Teresa of Portugal.

18 JUNE

In 1815 the Battle of Waterloo takes place: the final destruction of Napoleon's second attempt at power after escaping from the Island of Elba. Arthur Wellesley, Duke of Wellington, is in command of 93,000 allied forces: British, Hanoverians, Dutch, Belgians, Brunswickers and Nassauers. He is ably supported by 117,000 Prussians under Marshal Gebhard von Blucher.

Also on this day, in 1942, Paul McCartney is born, later to form the most successful pop group of all time, The Beatles.

Elizabeth of Schönau, Mark and Marcellian who were twins and martyred together.

19 JUNE

—«◉»—

In 1215, the Magna Carta is reluctantly sealed by King John. It limits the absolute power of the king and gives more power to his barons. Clause 39 has a wider application than they anticipate and becomes a fundamental precept of British law: 'No freeman shall be arrested or imprisoned or dispossessed or outlawed or banished or in any way molested, nor will we go upon him, nor send upon him, except by lawful judgement of his peers and the law of the land.'

On this day in 1566, James VI of Scotland is born, the child of Mary Queen of Scots and Lord Darnley. With Queen Elizabeth of England dying childless, he becomes king of both Great Britain and Ireland.

Boniface of Querfurt, Gervase and Protase, whose bodies were found as the result of a vision by St. Ambrose. Also the feast day of Juliana Falconieri and Romuald.

20 JUNE

In 1837, William IV dies in the night. The Lord Chamberlain and the Archbishop of Canterbury rush through the gardens to knock on the door of Kensington Palace, where eighteen-year-old Victoria is sleeping. The Lord Chamberlain kneels, kisses her hand and utters the words: 'Your Majesty' at which point she knows the throne is hers. She is crowned eight days later on 28 June.

 Adalbert of Magdeburg.

21 JUNE

Midsummer's Day – the longest day of the year in Britain. In Australia, this is the shortest day of the year.

On this day in 1813, the Battle of Vitoria is fought in Spain between Wellington's forces and those of Marshal Jourdan and Napoleon's brother Joseph. It is a resounding victory for Wellington and effectively ends Napoleon Bonaparte's power in Spain.

Also on this day in 1972, Hal Iggulden is born.

SUMMER SOLSTICE

LONGEST DAY

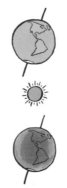

 Aloysius.

22 JUNE

In 1377, Richard II becomes King of England on the death of Edward III. He is ten years old. He is formally crowned in Westminster Abbey on 16 July 1377. His portrait, the oldest surviving contemporary painting of a monarch, hangs in the nave of that ancient church.

Also on this day, in 1937, the boxer Joe Louis becomes heavyweight world champion, knocking out Jim Braddock. He had only ever been beaten by one man in his career – Max Schmeling, cast by Nazi propaganda as an ideal Aryan warrior. Joe Louis said he would not consider himself champion until he had fought Schmeling again. A year after winning the title, he did. When Schmeling went down in the first round, Goebbels ordered the transmission to Germany to be cut off. Joe Louis won a convincing victory, though Germany didn't see it. Louis held the title for eleven years, eight months and nine days, the longest heavyweight reign to date.

The feast day of St. Alban, a Romano-Briton and the first British martyr. The feast day is shared with St. John Fisher and St.Thomas More, both men of great faith and learning who were executed by King Henry VIII. Also Nicetus of Remesiana and Paulinus of Nola.

23 JUNE

In 1757, the Battle of Plassey takes place, part of the Seven Years' War. Robert Clive, later known as 'Clive of India', is outnumbered many times, fighting the forces of the Nawab of Bengal and French artillerymen. Despite the odds, Clive pulls off an incredible victory, helping to secure the British in India and denying the French their claim.

 Audrey, Joseph Cafasso.

24 JUNE

The feast day of St John the Baptist and the second English Quarter Day, when rents became due. Two Sheriffs are elected by City Livery Companies in London on this day each year, although they don't take office until 28 September. Their duties are to aid the Lord Mayor of London, who has to attend the Central Criminal Court and present petitions to Parliament.

On this day in 1340, the Battle of Sluys takes place at sea, the first great battle of the Hundred Years' War against the French. The fleet is personally led by Edward III, who will go on to win the Battle of Crécy six years later, supporting his claim to France and establishing sovereignty over the English channel. Despite roughly equal numbers of ships, the French fleet are annihilated.

This day is also known as Bannockburn Day, after the battle in 1314, where Robert the Bruce clobbered the English forces under Edward II.

 John the Baptist, who baptised Jesus in the river Jordan.

25 JUNE

On this day in 1876, General George Armstrong Custer is killed at the Battle of Little Bighorn in Montana – otherwise known as Custer's Last Stand. Custer's 200 cavalrymen were massively outnumbered by around 2000 warriors from the Lakota, Sioux, Crow and Cheyenne tribes, led by Sitting Bull and Crazy Horse of the Lakota. In America and Britain, the event sparked popular imagination as a classic heroic tragedy of the wild west.

 Febronia, Prosper of Reggio.

26 JUNE

In 1917, embarrassed by family links to Germany in the middle of a war with them, King George V changes his surname from Saxe-Coburg-Gotha to Windsor, after the castle.

 Anthelm, John and Paul, early martyrs who died together.

27 JUNE

In 1746, after the failed second Jacobite Rebellion in 1745 and the disastrous Battle of Culloden, Bonnie Prince Charlie escapes to the Isle of Skye dressed as a maid.

Cyril of Alexandria, Ladislas.

28 JUNE

In 1491, Henry VIII is born. Famously, he goes on to have six wives, their fates remembered with this mnemonic: Divorced, beheaded, died, divorced, beheaded, survived. He becomes so enormously fat that by 1544, he has to be carried in a chair and can only move upstairs with a system of ropes and pulleys. He is buried in St George's Chapel, Windsor.

Also on this day, in 1914, Archduke Franz Ferdinand is assassinated at Sarajevo, beginning a domino sequence of events that ended in World War I.

Austol, the great theologian Iraneus, Vincentia Gerosa.

29 JUNE

The feast day of St Peter the apostle, who is meant to hold the keys to heaven. He is the patron saint of butchers, bakers and clock makers. His bones are in St Peter's Church in Rome.

Peter and Paul. Peter was leader of the apostles and the first Pope who admitted the first Gentile to Baptism. Paul was born Saul, but converted to Christianity on the road to Damascus and became a fervent supporter and writer.

30 JUNE

On this day in 1980, the silver sixpence is no longer legal tender

Martyrs of Rome, Theobald of Provins, George the Hagirote.

These are the days when birds come back,

A very few, a bird or two,

To take a backward look.

These are the days when skies resume

The old, old sophistries of June,

A blue and gold mistake.

Oh, fraud that cannot cheat the bee,

Almost thy plausibility

Induces my belief,

Till ranks of seeds their witness bear,

And softly through the altered air

Hurries a timid leaf!

Oh, sacrament of summer days,

Oh, last communion in the haze,

Permit a child to join,

Thy sacred emblems to partake,

Thy consecrated bread to break,

Taste thine immortal wine!

Emily Dickinson

SUMMER

A British summer lasts from mid June to mid September. It is a time for sports like tennis, and long evenings stretching into a grey twilight that gently meets the dark. The fields are full of golden wheat and the trees hang heavy with fruit. The drone of lawns being mowed is the sound of summer, while children climb trees and fall into ponds. Dogs smell of cut grass in summer and walking them is no longer a chore.

In greengrocers and supermarkets you'll find all the domestic fruits and vegetables in summer. Peas in the pod can be eaten without cooking them. Asparagus can be boiled in bundles of a dozen spears for 3–6 minutes, then served with butter and shavings of parmesan cheese, or alternatively with a poached egg. If you roast them (for around ten minutes), drizzle a little olive oil over them first. They are delicious.

Victoria Plums, gooseberries, strawberries and greengages also become available for the first time in this season. If you can find a place near you, it's a lot of fun to pick your own strawberries, especially for children. With controlled atmospheric storage and imported crops, these fruits are available all year round, but domestic crops will have been stored for shorter times and are likely to contain fewer, if any, chemicals. In general, the fresher the better, so it makes sense to go for fruit and vegetables that are locally produced where possible. Many varieties of British apples have been lost in the face of foreign competition, but in general are far better tasting than anything that has travelled far or been frozen. If you've ever had an apple with almost no flavour at all, it has almost certainly been kept at a very low temperature for up to a year before you bought it. Farmers' markets are growing in popularity

and supply a huge range of fresh local food of good quality.

Feasts and festivals of summer include: Glastonbury music festival in June, Father's Day on the third Sunday in June, the feast day of St Peter and St Paul on 29 June, the Durham Miners' Gala on the second or third Saturday in July, St Swithin's day on 15 July, Armada Day on 19 July, and the feast day of St Christopher on 25 July. The Highland Games take place in Scotland in summer. They involve famous events like Tossing the Caber, Tug of War, Piping and Highland Dancing.

Other events include the Whitstable Oyster Festival on the Saturday nearest to 25 July, Swan-Upping on the Thames,

the Grand Wardmote of the Woodmen of Arden in the first week of August, Notting Hill Carnival over the August Bank Holiday, Cromwell Day on 3 September and harvest festivals in churches and schools in late September, ending the season.

The summer solstice usually falls on 21 June, when the sun rises around 5 a.m. for a day that is eighteen hours long. It is either the beginning of summer, or its height, depending on how you look at such things. From now on, the days will begin to shorten as we head towards the autumn equinox on 22 or 23 September, when night and day are once more of equal length.

JULY

To early Romans, this month would have been 'Quintilis', the fifth month of the year before they added January and February. After Julius Caesar's death in 44 BC, Mark Antony had it renamed in his honour.

It was Julius Caesar who created the first calendar of 365 days, with an extra day every four years. He was aided in this task by the Greek astrologer Sosigenes. Caesar is also the one who arranged the days of each month into the pattern we know today: '30 days hath September, April, June and November. All the rest have thirty-one, except for February, which has twenty-eight days clear and twenty-nine each leap year.' It's a rotten poem, but it does help to remember them. Despite the best efforts of Caesar and Sosigenes, there was still some lack of accuracy and 'calendar drift' that had to be put right by the Gregorian reform in the sixteenth century.

Perhaps the most famous old custom in July is 'Swan-Upping', which has been going on for more than five hundred years. It stems from the fact that the queen does not own all the swans in Britain. Permission to keep and raise swans, then a delicacy, was given to the Worshipful Company of Vintners and the Company of Dyers around 1473. They are the only other private owners of swans. Since that time, the swan-keepers for those companies meet the Royal Swan Master in late July and travel down the Thames. Each young swan is marked with a single nick on the beak for the Dyers, or two nicks for the Vintners. Unmarked cygnets belong to the Queen.

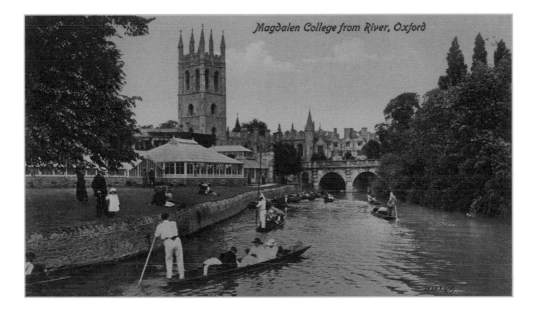

Magdalen College from River, Oxford

St Swithin's Day is on 15 July, which gives us this old rhyme: 'St Swithin's day, if thou dost rain, For forty days it will remain; St Swithin's day, if thou be fair, For forty days twill rain nae mair.'

The end of July heralds the 'Dog days', the hottest of the year, when dogs might run mad and Sirius, the Dog Star, rises in the sky with the sun.

The BBC prom concerts begin in July at the Royal Albert Hall in London, continuing to the famous 'Last Night of the Proms' in September.

TRADITIONAL CUSTOMS

Ebernoe Horn Fair
The Ebernoe Horn Fair takes place on 25 July in a small village in Sussex. A sheep is roasted and a game of cricket played. The player who scores the most runs is given a set of sheep's horns as the trophy. The presentation is accompanied by the Horn Fair Song.

Whitstable Oyster Festival
On the Saturday nearest to 25 July, the Whitstable Oyster festival is held. The first catch of the season is landed and followed by the 'oyster parade' in which oysters are delivered by horse-drawn cart to restaurants in the town.

Walking Day, Cheshire
On the first Friday in July, Warrington in Cheshire holds a Walking Day, where Guides, Scouts, local churches and organisations parade through the town with banners, accompanied by various marching bands. Around four thousand people are expected to take part each year.

Medway Admiralty Court
On the first Saturday in July, the 'Medway Admiralty Court' takes place in Kent, as it has done since 1446. The Mayor of Medway takes to the river on a decorated barge and from that position presides over a court of Aldermen and freemen allowed to fish the river. A freeman is someone who has served seven years as apprentice in that craft. In 2004, there were twenty-two. The Admiralty Court regulates the boundaries of the oyster beds and the amounts to be taken each season.

Michaelmas

One tradition for Michaelmas is the eating of a goose, once universal. In a similar fashion to the Italian belief that eating a pig's trotter and lentils will bring wealth, eating a goose was meant to bring financial security for the next year. An even older tradition suggests that it is unlucky to eat blackberries after this day, as the devil wipes himself with them. Why the devil would want to risk thorns getting stuck in sensitive places is never explained.

Little Edith's Treat, Piddenhoe

On 19 July, children in Piddenhoe, East Sussex benefit from an investment made in 1868. In that year, Elizabeth Croft's only granddaughter Edith died at just a few months old. To commemorate the little girl, her grandmother invested £100 with the instruction that the interest be used to treat local children on Edith's birthday each year. Known as 'Little Edith's Treat', the custom continues to this day, though the money is sometimes used to fund a Christmas party for local children instead.

Oxenhope Straw Race, Yorkshire

In early July, the Oxenhope Straw Race takes place, a fund-raising event for charity in Oxenhope, West Yorkshire, a tradition that stretches all the way back to 1975. Teams of two must carry a bale of hay around the course, drinking a pint of beer at five different pubs. All are welcome to have a go. Since its inception, the event has raised more than a quarter of a million pounds for local charities.

1 JULY

In 1868, Dominion Day for Canada came into being, established by statute in 1879. After 1982, this day became known as 'Canada Day'.

 Oliver Plunket, Simeon Salus.

2 JULY

In 1644, the Battle of Marston Moor is fought, the first major battle of the English Civil War between the forces of Parliament and King Charles I. It is a victory for the Roundheads – the parliamentary forces under Cromwell.

 Oudoceus, Bernardino Realino.

3 JULY

In 1940, after the creation of the Vichy French government who supported the Nazis, the British government could no longer trust that French ships would not fall into German hands, so on this day part of the French fleet is sunk in port at Mers el-Kebir in Algeria by the Royal Navy.

Pope Leo II. In addition, this is the feast day of Thomas the Apostle, perhaps best known as 'Doubting Thomas' as he refused to believe in the resurrection until he had seen the actual wounds.

4 JULY

In 1776 the Declaration of Independence is made by the United States, separating from Britain after more than a year of war. It is still known as 'Independence Day' in the US. The war goes on for another seven years until 1783. In that year, Cornwallis, the English military commander, hoped to escape a tightening noose of American forces. He was prevented from doing so by a French naval blockade. Famously, his military band played 'The World Turned Upside Down' as he surrendered. To celebrate their part in the war, the French later gave the Statue of Liberty to America.

 Andrew of Crete, Odo the Good, Ulric of Augsburg.

5 JULY

In 1996, Dolly, the world's first cloned sheep, is born, though her existence is kept secret until February 1997. In fact, previous clones had been created from embryonic cells, but Dolly is the first mammal to be created from adult cells. In theory, Elvis could be reborn in the same way.

 Athanasius the Athonite, Modwenna, Philomena of San Severino

6 JULY

In 1535, Lord Chancellor Sir Thomas More is executed in London for treason, having refused to accept Henry VIII as head of the Church of England. He is later canonised in 1935 on the 400th anniversary of his martyrdom. Robert Bolt's play *A Man for All Seasons* is a superb examination of the characters and arguments involved.

Godelive, Maria Goretti, Moninne, Sexburga

7 JULY

In 1967, after completing his single-handed voyage around the world, Sir Francis Chichester is knighted on this day by Queen Elizabeth II. Sir Francis Drake was knighted in the same way by Elizabeth I, after his own circumnavigation. Queen Elizabeth II used the same sword, recognising the historical parallel.

 Ethelburga of Faremoutiers-en-Brie, Prosper of Aquitaine, Willibald.

8 JULY

In 1889, John L. Sullivan defeats Jake Kilrain after a 75-round bare-knuckle heavyweight boxing match. Sullivan vomits in the forty-fourth round, but recovers to win. He is the last bare-knuckle champion. Later champions fight under the rules devised by the Marquis of Queensbury, with gloves.

Elizabeth of Portugal, Procopius.

9 JULY

In 1922, the American swimmer Johnny Weissmuller becomes the first person to swim 100 metres in less than a minute. He goes on to set more than sixty swimming world records and win five Olympic golds. He is, however, more famous for playing Tarzan in twelve films, beginning with Tarzan the Ape Man. In those, he is often seen swimming and wrestling with alligators. His ululating Tarzan yell is so good that it is used in later films with other actors.

Veronica Giuliani.

10 JULY

In 1553, the tragic Lady Jane Grey is proclaimed Queen. She is the granddaughter of Henry VIII's sister and this attempt to take the crown is arranged by the Duke of Northumberland. Lady Jane Grey is married to his son, Lord Dudley. Although she is declared the official heir by a dying Edward VI, neither Lords nor Commons would accept her over Mary I, Henry VIII's oldest daughter. Lady Jane reigns for only nine days. She and her husband are both beheaded on 12 February 1554

 Alexander and six other sons of St. Felicity, Antony of the Caves.

11 JULY

In 1274, Robert the Bruce is born at Turnberry Castle, Ayrshire, Scotland. He doesn't do too well against Edward I, but wins the Battle of Bannockburn against the English king's son, Edward II.

 Benedict, Olga.

12 JULY

In 1794, Admiral Horatio Nelson loses his right eye at the Siege of Calvi in Corsica. For a while, it looked as though the French were taking him a piece at a time.

Also on this day, Julius Caesar is born, c. 100 BC, back when it was the fifth month of the Roman calendar and known as Quintilis. The name of the month was later changed in his honour.

John the Iberian, John Gualbert, Veronica, who pressed a cloth against the face of Christ when she saw his suffering

13 JULY

In 1643, the Battle of Roundway Down is fought during the English Civil War. It was a Royalist cavalry success that formed part of the 'Royalist summer', where everything seemed to be going Charles I's way for a time.

 Eugenius of Carthage, Francis Solano, Silas.

14 JULY

In 1867, Alfred Nobel demonstrates dynamite for the first time in a Surrey quarry. Although the explosive is based on nitroglycerin, the huge advantage it has over that substance is that it could be roughly handled or even dropped without going off. Nobel combined nitroglycerin with clay and a pinch of sodium carbonate, forming the mixture into short sticks with fuses. Later in life, he will use his fortune to endow the Nobel prizes.

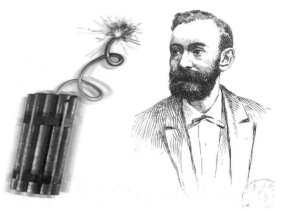

Nicodemus of the Holy Mountain, Phocas, Ulric of Zell.

15 JULY

St Swithin's Day. When St Swithin's bones were moved to a shrine in Winchester Cathedral on this day in 971 AD, it rained for the next forty days.

Bonaventure, Donald, Edith of Polesworth and Edith of Tamworth, James of Nisibis.

16 JULY

In 1969, *Apollo 11* launches in the first attempt to put a man on the moon. The historic crew is Neil Armstrong, Edwin 'Buzz' Aldrin and Michael Collins. They will reach the moon four days later, on 20 July.

Helier, Mary Madgalen Postel, Raineld.

17 JULY

In 2000, Tesco announces that it will revive imperial weights and measures in its shops after a survey discovers that nine out of ten customers think in those measures before buying. Both metric and imperial will be used from that point. Tim Mason, Tesco's marketing director, says, 'We are not anti-Europe. We are pro-shopper.' Over the next few years, it goes on to be the most successful supermarket chain in the UK.

 Kenelm, Narses of Lampron. The martyrs of Sicily.

18 JULY

In 1921, John Glenn, the American astronaut, is born. He will go on to be the fifth man in space and a US Senator. By 2007 he is still the oldest man to have gone into space, reaching orbit in 1998 at the age of 77.

Symphorosa and her seven sons, all of whom were martyred.

19 JULY

On this day in 1588, the Spanish Armada is sighted off the south coast. The attack that follows will lead to the most famous naval victory in English history. Ever since, this date has been known as Armada Day.

Also on this day, in 1799, the Rosetta stone is found by a French army engineer. As the Napoleonic war is going on, the British take it from him and transport it to London. Before the find, hieroglyphics were a mystery. Luckily, the Ptolemaic dynasty of Alexandria had descended from one of Alexander the Great's generals, Ptolemy. As a result, the stone is marked with a Greek translation and so hieroglyphics are understood for the first time. The phrase 'Rosetta stone' has come to mean anything that provides a key to sudden, illuminating understanding.

 Arsenius, Macrina the Younger.

20 JULY

In 1969, Neil Armstrong steps onto the moon surface in the Sea of Tranquility, saying, 'One small step for man, one giant leap for mankind.' Recently, it has been suggested that he *did* say 'a man' as he intended to, but the extra word was lost in a poor signal. Fair enough. The moon was further away than we had ever been before, after all. Buzz Aldrin followed him and Michael Collins was the third member of the team, remaining on board.

Elijah, Jerome Emiliani, Wilgefortis.

21 JULY

In 1403, the Battle of Shrewsbury takes place, between the Lancastrian king Henry IV and a rebel army led by members of the Percy family from Northumberland. It is chiefly remembered as the climax of Shakespeare's play, Henry IV, Part I.

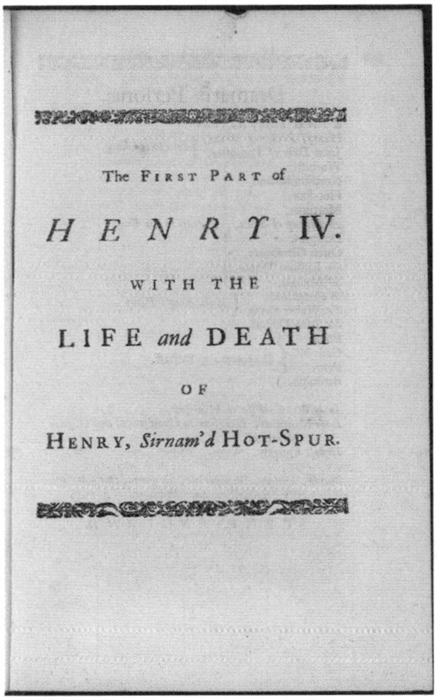

The First Part of

HENRY IV.

WITH THE

LIFE and DEATH

OF

HENRY, *Sirnam'd* HOT-SPUR.

Lawrence of Brindisi, Victor of Marseilles.

22 JULY

In 1812, the Battle of Salamanca takes place in Spain. Wellington had intended to pull back to Portugal after six weeks of tactical sparring with French forces under Marshal Marmont. When he sees a gap open on Marmont's left flank, Wellington shouts, 'By God, that will do!' and orders an attack. The victory is a crucial step in the Napoleonic wars. A French general commented of Wellington: 'He manoeuvred like Frederick the Great, in oblique order.'

Mary Magdalen, who was present both at the crucifixion and at the tomb, finding it empty.

In 1916, Sir William Ramsay dies in Buckinghamshire. Ramsay won the Nobel Prize for Chemistry in 1904 for discovering the noble gases argon, neon, krypton and xenon. He was also the first person to isolate helium.

In 1567, Mary Queen of Scots is forced to abdicate in favour of her son, James. A Catholic cousin to England's Elizabeth I, Mary's life was a tragic one. After a failed rebellion against Elizabeth, she was imprisoned for eighteen years and eventually tried on charges of treason. At her trial, she said: 'Remember, gentlemen, the Theatre of History is wider than the Realm of England.' Unlike the clean stroke that beheaded Anne Boleyn, it took three blows to remove Mary's head. When Elizabeth I died without heirs, Mary's son united the thrones as James I of England and VI of Scotland.

 Bridget, John Cassian.

 Boris and Gleb, Christine.

25 JULY

c.250 AD Feast day of St Christopher. The Vatican removed this feast day from the official list in 1969, which is a bit of a shame. St Christopher was said to be an enormously strong Roman named Reprobus. Reprobus asked a Christian hermit how he could serve Jesus. The man directed him to a fast-flowing stream, where Reprobus met a child asking to be carried across. The child became heavier and heavier, revealing that he was the child Jesus and his weight was the weight of the sins of the world. The boy then baptised Reprobus in the river, naming him 'Christopher', which means 'Christ-Carrier' in Greek. Despite his drop in official status, Christopher is still the patron saint of travellers and lorry drivers. In some parts of England, it is believed that seeing his image protects you against sudden or accidental death.

On this day in 1797, Admiral Nelson is grievously wounded in his right arm as he leads a disastrous assault on the Spanish city of Santa Cruz in Tenerife. A musket ball shatters the bone and opens a major artery. To save his life, the arm is amputated without anaesthetic on board HMS *Theseus*.

Christopher, James the Greater, apostle and brother to John.

In 1894, Aldous Huxley is born. His most famous novel is *Brave New World*. Another book, *The Doors to Perception*, details the author's experience with mescaline, a hallucinogenic drug. The title comes from a line of Blake's poetry: 'If the doors of perception were cleansed, everything would appear to man as it is: infinite.' The title is later used by Jim Morrison to name his group 'The Doors'.

Joachim and Ann, Bartholomea Capitanio.

In 1586, English explorer Sir Walter Ralegh brings tobacco back to England from Virginia, the American state. It would become a major cash crop. There is a story that when Ralegh's servant first saw him smoking it, he threw a bucket of water over his master to 'put him out'. Ralegh is also credited with bringing potatoes to England and Ireland for the first time, though this may be apocryphal.

Aurelius and Natalia, Clement Slovensky, Pantaleon. This is also the feast day of the seven sleepers, men walled up who are said to have lived again when they were revealed centuries later.

28 JULY

In 2004, Francis Crick (seen with Watson below) dies in San Diego. With James Watson and Maurice Wilkins, he was the discoverer of the DNA helix. The three men shared the Nobel Prize for Physiology or Medicine in 1962.

Also on this day, in 2006, David Gemmell dies, aged only 56. He was a superb writer of heroic fantasy fiction.

Nazarius and Celsus, Samson.

In 1588, the Spanish Armada's attempt to invade England and restore Catholicism is defeated. The Spanish King, Philip, sent 130 ships to land in Portsmouth, but they are broken by better seamanship and gunnery off the coast of Dorset and the Isle of Wight. Over the next few weeks, the remnants of the Armada are scattered by fireships and then pursued all the way north to Scotland before the chase is called off.

Also on this day, in 1954, *The Fellowship of the Ring*, the first in *The Lord of the Rings* trilogy by J. R. R. Tolkien, is published in the UK. The trilogy will go on to be extraordinarily successful.

Lupus of Troyes, Martha, Olaf.

THE FELLOWSHIP OF THE RING

J. R. R. TOLKIEN

30 JULY

In 1966, England wins the World Cup, beating Germany 4–2 at Wembley Stadium. It was 2–2 at the end of normal time, then in extra time Geoff Hurst scored a controversial goal, causing much debate as to whether it crossed the goal line or not. It did, though, so that's enough of that. Hurst scored again in the final minute. The BBC commentator, Kenneth Wolstenholme, said famously, 'Some people are on the pitch. They think it's all over…it is now! It's four!'

Justin de Jacobis, Peter Chrysologus.

31 JULY

In 1910, the infamous Dr Crippen is arrested at sea for the murder of his wife. He is the first criminal to be caught by the use of radio and is later hanged at Pentonville Prison.

Germanus of Auxerre, Ignatius of Loyola, Neot.

AUGUST

For early Romans, this month would have been 'Sextilis', the sixth month. Now, of course, it is the eighth, with January and February added in. Not to be outdone by the month named for his great-uncle Julius, Augustus Caesar named August after himself. His true name was Octavian, but he took the title 'Augustus', meaning noble and impressive. He was a great emperor, but not a modest one.

In Britain, 1 August is the feast of Lammas, a popular time for fairs and festivals such as those at Exeter and York. It is also the feast day of 'St Peter ad Vincula', or 'St Peter in Chains', commemorating the time he was visited by an angel while languishing in prison and the chains fell from his hands.

The first of the month is also known as 'Minden Day', after the battle of Minden in the Seven Years' War – the true first world war in many ways and the most successful in British history, which is saying something. On this day in 1759, a vastly outnumbered column of British infantry routed eleven squadrons of French cavalry, an incredible feat of arms. It is still celebrated by the regiments who had men in that mixed column. As the British column advanced, they passed through a garden and took roses to wear in their hats. On this day each year, 'Minden Roses' are worn by serving and retired men of the Suffolk regiment, the Royal Hampshire, the Lancashire Fusiliers, The Royal Welsh Fusiliers, the King's Own Yorkshire Light Infantry and the King's Own Scottish Borderers.

At the other end of the month, we have St Bartholemew's Day on the 24 August, which used to signal the beginning of Bartholomew Fair in London, one of the great annual festivals from the twelfth century to late in the eighteenth. At its height, it catered for all tastes and involved prize-fights, gambling, drink, song, theatre, dance, acrobats, prostitution and just about anything else you could imagine wanting to try while in London.

The last Sunday of the month is still sometimes known as 'Plague Sunday', commemorating the extraordinary sacrifice of the village of Eyam (pronounced 'Eem') in Derbyshire. The Black Death of 1665 reached them in September of that year. The local rector, William Mompesson, persuaded the villagers to impose a strict quarantine on Eyam to stop the spread of the disease. They succeeded and none of the villages around them were touched. In Eyam itself, by the time the plague passed, 260 of 350 families had died.

August is the end of summer, with autumn just around the corner. Harvest whatever you've been growing in your garden and eat or freeze whatever won't keep. Later in the year, it is a wonderful thing to thaw your own veg and make a winter soup by boiling them in water with a little chicken stock, white wine, butter, and salt and pepper to taste. Apple-picking begins in August for orchards in the southern counties of Devon and Somerset. Greengages and plums ripen at around the same time.

TRADITIONAL CUSTOMS

St Bartholomew's Day, Kent
St Bartholomew's Day is on 24 August. On this day, there is a special service at the chapel of the Hospital of St Bartholomew in Sandwich, Kent. Adults are given biscuits stamped with the crest of the town and children are given buns after they have run all the way round the chapel.

Notting Hill Carnival, London
Notting Hill Carnival in London has its climax on the August Bank Holiday Monday. One and a half million people go to see the exotic costumes in the parade, which stretches for three miles. It may be the biggest street party in the world, which is saying something when you think of the Brazilian Mardi Gras.

Rush-bearing, Cumbria
There are five places in Cumbria that maintain the tradition of 'Rush-bearing', a procession through the town by local congregations carrying rushes formed into symbolic shapes. Grasmere is the most famous, perhaps because it was once a favourite of William Wordsworth and his sister Dorothy, who lived in the town and helped to keep this attractive summer tradition alive. The procession is led by six young girls, the 'Rush Maidens', who carry rushes to the church, beginning a day of celebration that ends with a dance in the evening.

St Nicholas' Church, Sutton

When Mary Gibson died in 1793, she was buried in St. Nicholas' church in Sutton, south London. She left money to have a sermon said and the tomb checked on 12 August, the anniversary of her death. Every year on this date, the Rector of the church formally opens and inspects the tomb.

Apple Pie Fair, Devon

Since 1888, the village of Marldon in Devon holds the Apple Pie fair on the August bank holiday Monday. As well as a village fete with stalls and a tug of war, a local baker makes a huge apple pie which is then drawn through the fete on a cart by a donkey. The donkey is accompanied to the Jubilee Meadow by the Apple Pie Princess, a local girl who makes the first cut.

Lammas Day

The first of August is Lammas day – an Anglican church festival of 'first fruits' going back to at least the ninth century. It was also a day for paying rent and settling debts, and an official Quarter Day in Scotland. The church festival has seen a revival since the 1940s.

Stag Hunting

On 1 August, the Red and Sika stag-hunting season begins in England and Wales, ending on 30 April. In Scotland, the season is from 1 July until 20 October.

1 AUGUST

On this day in 1798, Nelson is victorious in the battle of the Nile. One of the French ships destroyed is Napoleon's flagship, *L'Orient*. Nelson collects some of the timbers and has them made into his coffin. Famously, he has to be pickled first in alcohol to keep him fresh for the trip home after Trafalgar. Legend has it that a good deal of the liquor had been drunk. Nelson's final tomb in St Paul's sits close to Wellington's and Admiral Collingwood's, Nelson's friend who commanded the Trafalgar fleet after Nelson's death.

On this day in 1907, the first experimental Boy Scout camp takes place. Founded by Robert Baden-Powell, the Scout movement celebrated their centenary in 2007. It was founded by Robert Baden-Powell, a hero of the Siege of Mafeking. There are currently 38 million members worldwide in more than two hundred countries. When girls turned up at a Boy Scout rally in 1909, calling themselves 'Girl Scouts', Baden-Powell created the Girl Guides, passing over the running to his sister Agnes.

Alphonsus Liguori, Ethelwold, Faith, Hope and Charity.

2 AUGUST

'In fourteen hundred and ninety two, Columbus sailed the ocean blue.' He was a hopeless explorer. On this day, he reaches America by accident. Believing it to be an island, he names it Santa Isla. Honestly, the man was an idiot.

Also on this day, in 1876, James Butler Hickok, better known as Wild Bill Hickok, is shot dead at a saloon in the town of Deadwood. He never usually played poker with his back to the door, but on this day there was no other seat. As Hickok picks up his cards, a man named Jack McCall enters and shoots him in the back of the head. The motive for the murder is uncertain, though it may have been rage born of humiliation. Hickok had offered to buy McCall breakfast after he had lost his money the previous day. The hand Hickok held was pairs of aces and eights, with the fifth card unknown. It is still called the Dead Man's hand. Before his death, he was a legendary sheriff and gunfighter of the old west.

 Basil the Blessed, Eusebius of Vercelli.

3 AUGUST

In 216 BC the Battle of Cannae, part of the Second Punic War, takes place. The exact date can never be absolutely certain, but the battle is fought in the high summer. It is one of the most crushing defeats ever endured by a Roman army. Hannibal, a Carthaginian general, had a mixed force of many nations. He was outnumbered by professional Roman soldiers and should have been easily routed. Instead, he adopted a cup formation, allowing his own front line to fall back and back until the entire Roman force was trapped and compressed inside the cup. Hannibal's cavalry were superb and held the Roman horse in stalemate while the slaughter continued. The Romans lost between fifty and sixty thousand men, one of the costliest battles in all history.

Peter Eymard.

4 AUGUST

In 1792, Percy Bysshe Shelley is born. One of the Romantic poets, he is best known for 'Ozymandias', and perhaps for the fact that his wife, Mary Shelley, wrote *Frankenstein*. Percy Shelley drowned in 1822, just before his thirtieth birthday. His heart was taken from his funeral pyre and given to his wife. His ashes are buried in the Protestant Cemetery, Rome.

On this day in 1900, Lady Elizabeth Bowes-Lyon, consort to George VI is born. She is later known as Queen Elizabeth the Queen Mother. She died in 2002 and is buried with her husband at St. George's Chapel, Windsor.

> *'My name is Ozymandias,*
>   *king of kings:*
> *Look on my works, ye Mighty,*
>   *and despair!'*
> *Nothing beside remains.*
>   *Round the decay*
> *Of that colossal wreck,*
>   *boundless and bare*
> *The lone and level sands*
>   *stretch far away.*
>   **Extract from 'Ozymandias'**
>   **by Shelley**

 John-Baptist Vianney.

5 AUGUST

In 1962, Marilyn Monroe, born Norma Jean Baker, is found dead at her home in California after an overdose of barbiturates in the form of sleeping pills. She was 36 years old.

Afra, Pope Sixtus II who was martyred with his companions.

6 AUGUST

In 1881, Alexander Fleming is born, discoverer of penicillin, the first general-purpose antibiotic. Others claim to have discovered it first, but history can be hard on the losers. Fleming died in 1955 and is buried in St Paul's Cathedral. Few lives have saved so many others.

Also on this day, in 1945, the first atomic bomb is dropped on Hiroshima, followed three days later by the bomb on Nagasaki. Japan's unconditional surrender followed on 14 August.

Sixtus.

7 AUGUST

In 1485, Henry Tudor, the Earl of Richmond who will later become King Henry VII, father to Henry VIII and grandfather to Elizabeth I, lands at Milford Haven to claim the English throne. It is not a particularly strong claim, but he beats Richard III at the Battle of Bosworth Field, ending any further argument. Richard is the last king of England to die on the battlefield.

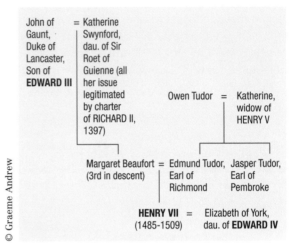

© Graeme Andrew

Dominic, founder of the Dominican monastic order.

8 AUGUST

In 1902, the theoretical physicist Paul Dirac is born in Bristol. He will go on to be one of the founders in the field of quantum physics and formulate the 'Dirac equation', which predicted the existence of anti-matter in the universe. He wins the Nobel Prize for Physics in 1933, sharing it with Erwin Schrödinger, a man most famous for his question about a cat in a box.

 Cajetan, Cyriacus, Hormidz.

9 AUGUST

In 480 BC, around this date (some sources suggest 17 August), King Leonidas and his Spartans are finally defeated by the Persian King Xerxes at the Pass of Thermopylae. 'Go tell the Spartans, stranger passing by, that here, obedient to their laws, we lie.' As well as the word 'Spartan', they also gave us the word 'laconic', as their region of Greece was known as Laconia. It means a brief, dry wit and comes from an exchange initiated by Philip of Macedon, father to Alexander the Great. He sent the message to the Spartans: 'If I enter Laconia, I will level Sparta to the ground.' They replied with a single word: 'If.'

Also on this day, in 1387, Henry V is born, who goes on to win the Battle of Agincourt.

 Oswald of Northumbria.

10 AUGUST

In 1675, Charles II lays the foundation stone for the Royal Observatory at Greenwich, London. It will later become the zero point for longitude, beginning the world's 24 noon time zones and beating Paris to the honour by a whisker.

 Lawrence, Philomena.

11 AUGUST

In 1897, Enid Blyton is born in London. She will go on to be the most famous children's author in history, with instantly recognisable creations such as *The Famous Five*, *The Secret Seven*, *The Magic Faraway Tree* and the *Noddy* stories. In all, she wrote around eight *hundred* books.

 Attracta, Clare of Assisi, Susan, Tiburtius.

12 AUGUST

Grouse-shooting season opens, ending on 10 December. The day is sometimes known as 'The Glorious Twelfth'.

On this day in 1762, George IV is born, the son of George III. He becomes king on his father's death in 1820, but because of his father's madness, is Prince Regent for nine years before that. His only daughter, Charlotte, dies with her child during childbirth, so the throne passes to George IV's brother, William IV. He too dies without heirs and the throne is passed to Queen Victoria, the eighteen-year-old daughter of another son of George III.

Also on this day, in 1949, the first Geneva Convention is signed.

 Jambert, Murtagh.

13 AUGUST

In 1415, Henry V lands at Harfleur in Normandy. He will fight the French knights at Agincourt two months later.

 Hippolytus of Rome, Maximus the Confessor, Narses the Gracious, Radegund, Tikhon of Zadonsk.

14 AUGUST

In 1945 Japan surrenders at last. VJ day (Victory over Japan) is celebrated on 15 August.

Maximilian Kolbe, who offered his life in exchange for a man with a family at Auschwitz concentration camp. The man he saved was present at his canonisation in 1982.

15 AUGUST

In 1888, T. E. Lawrence is born, later known as Lawrence of Arabia. He goes on to become an archaeologist, linguist, writer, adviser to a young Winston Churchill, soldier and pilot. He dies aged 46 in a motorcycle accident and is buried in St Paul's Cathedral.

The Blessed Virgin Mary (Assumption), Tarcisius.

16 AUGUST

In 1977, Elvis Presley dies of a heart attack induced by barbiturates at his home in Memphis. He starred in thirty successful films and made 81 albums, all of which went from gold (500,000 copies sold) to triple triple platinum (nine million sold). From those, 53 singles were taken, with similar sales. He is the most successful recording artist in history by a huge margin.

 Stephen of Hungary.

17 AUGUST

In 1896, Mrs Bridget Driscoll, aged 44, becomes Britain's first pedestrian to be killed by a car, despite being hit at approximately 4 mph. She froze in shock on seeing the car and suffered a fatal head injury as she fell. At her inquest, coroner Percy Morrison said he hoped 'such a thing would never happen again'.

Hyacinth of Cracow, Mamas.

18 AUGUST

In 1227, Genghis Khan dies at the age of 55 after falling from a horse, though the date is not absolutely certain. Legends persist that he was stabbed by a woman and eventually lost too much blood to stay in the saddle. In his life, he conquered an area four times larger than that gained by Alexander the Great. His ruthlessness is legendary, though much of that image comes from history written by those he conquered. In Mongolia he is considered the heroic father of a nation. His sons went on to enlarge his empire, and his grandson, Kublai, became emperor of a united China.

Florus and Laurus, Helen.

19 AUGUST

In 1819, James Watt dies. He developed and improved early types of steam engine, creating the form that would become the workhorse of the world. He was the first to use the term 'horsepower' and the unit of power, a 'watt', is named after him.

Arnulf of Metz, John Eudes.

20 AUGUST

In 1913, Harry Brearley casts the first stainless steel, an alloy of iron and 12 per cent chromium that resists corrosion.

Amadour, Bernard of Clairvaux, Oswin.

21 AUGUST

In 1808, Wellington, with an Anglo-Portuguese force, defeats the French under General Jean Junot, in the Battle of Vimeiro in Portugal, part of the Peninsular War. Two thousand French soldiers are killed during the short battle. Wellington accepts Junot's surrender and then uses the Royal Navy to transport the French survivors home, even allowing them to keep valuables they had looted. His unusual generosity makes him the subject of an inquiry into his conduct. He is eventually exonerated, but in his absence command passes to Sir John Moore, who is killed at Corunna in 1809.

 Abraham of Smolensk, Sidonius Apollinaris.

In 1771, Henry Maudslay is born at the Woolwich Arsenal. His is an almost forgotten name of British engineering history. He goes on to invent the first bench micrometer capable of measuring one ten-thousandth of an inch and becomes an expert in industrial machinery, developing the precision screw-cutting lathe. He completes huge commissions for Marc Isambard Brunel, father to the more famous Isambard Kingdom Brunel. He also trains many men who make great strides in engineering themselves, including Joseph Clement, who produces the precision machinery for Charles Babbage's 'difference engine', and James Nasmyth, who invents the steam hammer and creates machine tools for Brunel's ship the SS *Great Britain*.

In 1305, in an *incredibly* brutal death, William Wallace, the Scottish war leader, is first part-hanged, then 'drawn', which means ripped open while still alive. He is then castrated, eviscerated, beheaded and his body cut into four pieces. His head is placed on a pike in London, joined by that of his brother John.

 Philip Benizi, Rose of Lima.

 Symphorian.

24 AUGUST

In 79 AD, the volcano Vesuvius erupts in southern Italy, burying the towns of Pompeii, Herculaneum and Stabiae under hot ash and boiling mud. Pompeii in particular is an extraordinary place to visit. Modern excavations revealed an almost intact ancient city, complete with graffiti, houses of ill-repute, a maze of streets, two theatres and a ring for gladiatorial games. There is nowhere quite like it in the world.

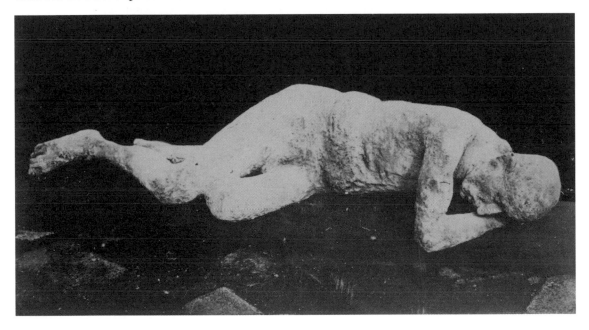

Bartholomew, Emily de Vialar, Joan Thouret.

25 AUGUST

In 1944, the Liberation of Paris by French forces takes place. France was actually liberated from the Nazis by American, Canadian and British forces. The French leader, De Gaulle spent the war in London, but insisted on being the first into Paris and is greeted with great joy on this day. He is also greeted with sniper fire from German soldiers and French fascists, but he is not hurt and American soldiers move in quickly to mop up the last of the resistance.

On this day in 2006, Andy Green, who set the world land speed record in the car *Thrust SSC* in 1997, drives the world's fastest diesel – the JCB Dieselmax – at the Bonneville salt flats in America, reaching a speed of 328 mph.

Genesius the Actor, Genesius of Arles, Gregory of Utrecht.

26 AUGUST

On this day in 1346, the Battle of Crécy takes place, one of the most important battles of the Hundred Years' War. Twelve thousand men under Edward III and his son, the Black Prince, take on 30–40,000 French. The English longbow triumphs. At one point, Edward is told that his sixteen-year-old son is hard pressed by the enemy. Should reinforcements be sent? He refuses, saying his son 'must win his spurs'. The Black Prince fights his way free unaided.

 Elizabeth Bichier des Ages.

27 AUGUST

In 1883, the volcano Krakatoa explodes in Indonesia. A resulting tsunami kills many thousands on Java and Sumatra. The resulting ash cloud is so vast that it drifts around the earth and causes particularly vivid sunsets for years afterwards.

 Caesarius of Arles, Monica.

In 1879, the Zulu king, Cetewayo kaMpande, is eventually captured by the British after the Battle of Ulundi earlier in the month. His capture marks the end of the Zulu wars, which included events like Isandlwana and Rorke's Drift. Cetshwayo is sent into exile and dies five years later. Zulu tribal lands become part of the union of South Africa, making Cetewayo the last independent Zulu King.

 Augustine of Hippo, Joaquina.

In 1831, Michael Faraday demonstrates the production of electricity from an induction ring. One of the great experimental scientists, he discovered that a copper disc rotating between the poles of a horseshoe magnet could produce a current on wires through the disc. This leads to the first electrical transformer and the first electric motor. A genius of the first order.

John the Baptist (feast day for his death by beheading).

30 AUGUST

In 1797, Mary Wollstonecraft Godwin is born, better known by her married name of Mary Shelley. She is most famous for her novel *Frankenstein*. A vegetarian herself, she also makes the monster of the book a vegetarian, which dampens down the horror somewhat. The thought of him clumping through the night after a nut cutlet doesn't create quite the terror you might expect.

Felix and Adauctus.

31 AUGUST

In 1888, Mary Ann Nichols, the first victim of Jack the Ripper, is found mutilated in Whitechapel, London. At least five other victims follow and the particularly grisly murders become famous throughout the world. Despite a number of theories as to his identity, the murderer is never caught.

On this day in 1997, Lady Diana Spencer and her lover Dodi Fayed die in Paris after a car crash in the early hours of the morning.

Aidan of Lindisfarne, Paullnus of Trier, Raymund Nonnatus.

SEPTEMBER

In Roman times, September was the seventh month, before the addition of January and February. This month sees the beginning of the oyster season around Colchester, a tradition that gained its charter in 1189 with the assent of Richard I. The season runs until April – all the months with the letter 'R' in them. Native oysters spawn from May to August and are not marketed in those months. In Colchester, the mayor and his companions go out in a boat for the first catch. On their return, they reread the original charter, drink gin and eat gingerbread with the oysters. After that, they send a message of loyalty to the queen.

After the harvests at the end of summer, anything left in your garden should be harvested this month, or it will be lost to pests and autumn cold. Anything like beans, peas or courgettes can be cut and frozen to eat later. This does not work with lettuces. Any fruit still remaining should be eaten. Raspberries go particularly well with vanilla ice-cream. There is an ancient tradition about not eating blackberries after Michaelmas on 29 September, and perhaps that stems from common sense.

The Lord Mayor of London is elected on 29 September each year. Candidates must be serving aldermen and have served as a city sheriff. The Lord Mayor then chairs the Council of Aldermen and the Court of the Common Council and becomes Admiral of the Port of London, Chief Magistrate of the City and Chancellor of City

University. In this way, it is far more than a merely ceremonial role. As well as the pantomime character of Dick Whittington and his clever cat, there really was a Lord Mayor named Richard Whittington who was elected to the post four times in the fifteenth century. Whether the real man had a cat cannot be said with any certainty.

Cider apples in southern counties are harvested in mid-September. Bats feed on the insects that eat ripe fruit, so can often be seen on still, warm evenings. Butterflies too feed on ripe plums and can be common at this time of year.

TRADITIONAL CUSTOMS

Bognor Birdman Competition

In the first week of September, the 'Bognor Birdman' competition takes place. It began in nearby Selsey in 1971, with a prize for anyone who could 'fly' for fifty yards without the aid of machinery. Considering it involves jumping off a pier in odd costumes, it's a lot of fun for the spectators. Some competitors do take it seriously and teams from many countries arrive to try and claim the prize of £25,000 for a hundred-metre flight.

Classic Races

The fifth English Classic race, the St Leger Stakes, is run in September at Doncaster Racecourse. It began in 1776. The Two Thousand Guineas, the Epsom Derby and the St Leger make up the Triple Crown of flat racing.

Crab-Apple Fair, Cumbria

The Egremont Crab-Apple Fair is held in Cumbria on the third Saturday in September. There you will find many activities lost elsewhere: gurning, climbing a greasy pole, tug of war and a pipe-smoking contest, to name just a few.

Carter's Steam Fair

Carter's Steam Fair comes to Croxley Green in Hertfordshire in mid-September. Many of the rides date back to the 1800s and are beautifully painted and preserved. On the same day, a classic car display is held with more than 800 vintage cars, vans and motorcycles.

Hop Picking

The long school summer holiday was originally designed to allow children in agricultural areas to help their parents gather in the crops. Up to quarter of a million hop-pickers were needed in Kent alone in the eighteenth century. These days, the work is mostly done by specialist picking machines, though some work is still available. The new term starts for all schools in the first week of September, to the utter relief of parents.

1 SEPTEMBER

Partridge-shooting season begins, ending on 1 February. Wild geese and duck may also be shot from this day until 20 February.

On this day in 1939, Nazi Germany under Adolf Hitler invades Poland with 1.5 million troops. The attack was unprovoked and began World War II, which would rage until 1945.

Fiacre, Giles.

2 SEPTEMBER

In 1666, the Great Fire of London begins at a baker's in Pudding Lane, burning for three days. The Royal Exchange, St Paul's Cathedral, prisons, hospitals, schools, bridges, churches and city gates are destroyed, as well as 400 streets and 13,200 houses. Despite having no organised fire service, astonishingly only nine people died. The one good thing about the fire is that it ended the bubonic plague outbreak of 1665. 'The Monument' is later raised to commemorate the fire, and many of the most important commissions to rebuild go to Christopher Wren, the greatest architect of the day.

 Brocard.

3 SEPTEMBER

In 1658, Oliver Cromwell, the Lord Protector of England, dies. Each year, the day of his death is commemorated with an open-air service near his statue in front of the Houses of Parliament, and a wreath laid at his feet.

On this day in 1939, the United Kingdom and France declare war on Germany, after the invasion of Poland two days before. France surrenders to Germany nine months later.

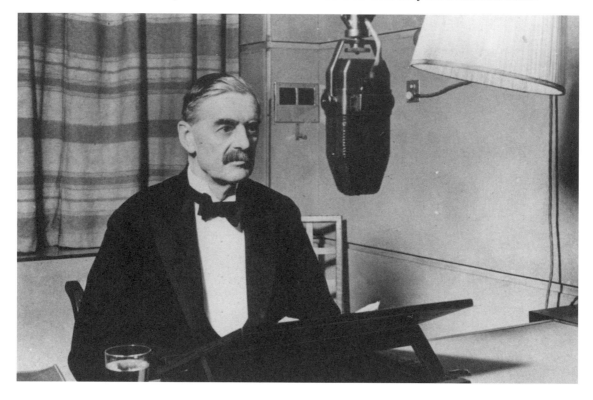

 Cuthburga, Pope Gregory the Great.

4 SEPTEMBER

In 476 AD, Flavius Romulus Augustus is deposed by the Germanic chieftain Odoacer. Romulus Augustus is the last of the Western Roman emperors, so this date is sometimes given as the end of the Roman Empire, though the Eastern Roman Empire around Constantinople survives for centuries after this date.

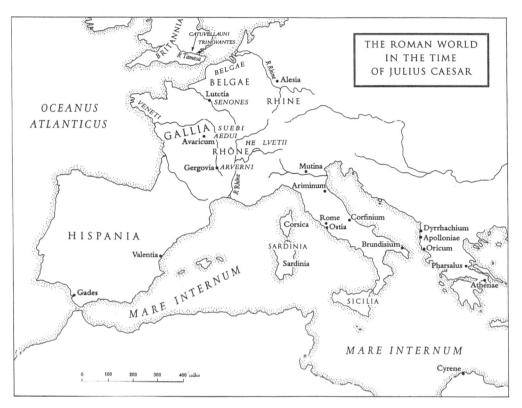

THE ROMAN WORLD
IN THE TIME
OF JULIUS CAESAR

 Marinus of San Marino.

5 SEPTEMBER

In 1781, the Battle of Chesapeake Capes takes place, part of the American War of Independence against the British. A French fleet under Admiral de Grasse fights the British fleet under Admiral Thomas Graves. Though the actual sea battle is not conclusive, it does have the effect of denying Cornwallis the support of the Royal Navy, leading to his eventual surrender to American forces at Yorktown.

Also on this day, in 1800, French forces surrender on Malta, after Nelson arrives in the area and prevents them being resupplied. They were already starving and had eaten all the dogs and cats in Valletta. With no way of feeding them, Nelson allowed the French soldiers to withdraw to Marseilles.

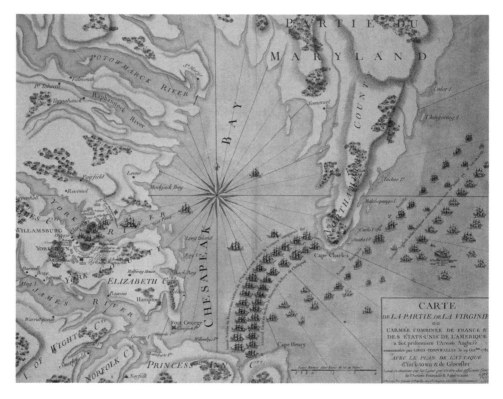

Lawrence Giustiniani.

6 SEPTEMBER

In 1620, the Pilgrim Fathers set sail for the Americas in the *Mayflower*. A Puritanical religious group, they had suffered in England and were looking for somewhere they could practise their faith. They had set out the day before in two ships, but the *Speedwell* leaked and had to dock at Plymouth in Devon. It is from Plymouth that the *Mayflower* finally leaves, landing at last on the east coast of North America. Once there, they seek out a suitable place to begin a colony and end up in a location they also name Plymouth, in Massachusetts. They are not the first English people to make the trip, nor are they the first successful colony, but they are by far the best known and have become part of American history, usually involving something to do with turkeys.

On this day in 1651, Charles II spends the night in an oak tree to avoid Cromwell's forces after losing the battle of Worcester. After Cromwell's death in 1658, Charles II is invited to take the throne in the Restoration, 1660, just in time for bubonic plague and the Great Fire of London.

Finally, on this day in 1666, the Great Fire of London is finally put out.

Afbeelding van de STADT LONDON. Representation curieuse de l'embrasement de la VILLE de LONDRES. CITIE LONDON. Delineation of the

 Bee, Cagnoald.

7 SEPTEMBER

In 1533, Elizabeth I is born, daughter to Henry VIII and Anne Boleyn. Imprisoned while her sister Mary ruled, she came to power in 1558 on Mary's death without heirs. The fact that neither sister had children is sometimes seen as evidence that their father Henry may have had syphilis, which sometimes leads to barren children. Elizabeth formally ratified the Church of England in 1563. From that point, English Catholics are persecuted with at almost as much fervour as Mary previously persecuted the Protestants before.

 Cloud, Evurtius.

8 SEPTEMBER

In 1157, Richard the Lionheart is born at Beaumont Palace. He is perhaps most famous for spending less than a year of his ten-year reign in England, spending the rest of the time on Crusades or imprisoned. Like his father, Henry II, Richard is buried in Fontrevault Abbey in France. It is not too surprising that his brother John tried to displace this absentee king. The story of Robin Hood comes from this period.

On this day in 1978, John Anthony Miller, better known as the author Peter Pook, dies. His books are hilarious.

Adrian, Ethelburga of Kent.

9 SEPTEMBER

In 1754, William Bligh is born in Plymouth. He is most famous for the mutiny on the *Bounty*, of which he was captain. The mutineers, under Fletcher Christian, abandoned Bligh and eighteen crew who had remained loyal in a 23-foot boat, with food and water for a few days, a sextant and a pocket watch. Tahiti was the closest destination, but Bligh wanted to get the news of the mutiny back to the Admiralty in England and he had learned navigation under Captain James Cook. In an astonishing feat of endurance and skill, Bligh navigated to Timor, 3,600 miles away. The journey took 41 days. Bligh was later exonerated of any blame in the mutiny and his reputation for cruelty may be undeserved in the context of the Royal Navy at that time.

Ciaran of Clonmacnois, Isaac the Great, Joseph of Volokolamsk.

In 1897, the first British drink-driving conviction is handed out. Driving a brand-new electric 'Horseless Carriage' taxi with a top speed of 9 mph, George Smith is fined a pound for driving first on the pavement and then into the front of 165 Bond Street in London. Electric taxis would later be withdrawn and the first petrol-engine ones licensed in 1903.

In 2001, two planes are flown into the World Trade Centre by Islamic extremists, killing around 3,000 people and causing the Twin Towers to collapse.

 Aubert of Avranches, Finnian of Moville, Nicholas of Tolentino.

Paphnutius, Protus and Hyacinth.

12 SEPTEMBER

In 2001, the United States declares war on terror as a result of the Twin Towers bombings.

 Guy of Anderlecht.

13 SEPTEMBER

In 1759, James Wolfe defeats the French at Quebec in Canada in the Seven Years' War, changing the history of a continent. Both he and the French commander die in the battle. Wolfe's navigator is James Cook, who will go on to discover Australia, the 'Terra Australis' that was the stuff of legend right up to him running a ship into it.

 Eulogius of Alexandria, John Chrystotum, Notburga.

14 SEPTEMBER

In 1959, the unmanned Soviet probe *Luna 2* crashes into the moon. It is the first human machine to reach the surface, with a hard landing that destroys *Luna 2* in the process.

 Albert of Jerusalem.

15 SEPTEMBER

Battle of Britain Day, celebrating the RAF victory at the beginning of World War II in 1940.

On this day in 1859, Isambard Kingdom Brunel dies, aged 53. He was responsible for many of the great Victorian engineering projects, including the Thames Tunnel and the Clifton Suspension Bridge.

Catherine of Genoa, Nicetas the Goth, Nicomedes.

'International Day for the Preservation of the Ozone Layer' Honestly, you could not make it up. It might be a good cause, but having a day for it is just ludicrous. You might as well have a day for 'Stopping Mugging' – and there probably is.

In 1787, the American Constitution is officially approved, including amendments. Having won the War of Independence against the British, America is launched onto the world scene. The American Bicentenary (two hundredth anniversary) was celebrated in 1976, taking the original date from the Declaration of Independence in 1776.

On this day in 1944, Operation Market Garden begins, which involves the mass landing of troops in Holland during World War Two. An armada of planes takes off from airbases all over England, towing gliders full of men and equipment. One of the Albermarles is flown by H.N. Iggulden.

Cornelius, Cyprian, Edith of Wilton, Ninian.

Columba of Cordoba, Hildegard, Lambert of Maastricht, Socrates.

18 SEPTEMBER

In 1709, Dr Samuel Johnson is born. He will go on to become a celebrated essayist, poet, wit and critic, much of his life recorded by his biographer James Boswell. Johnson is best known for *A Dictionary of the English Language*, which he wrote over nine years. One of the better known definitions from it is: 'Lexicographer: A writer of dictionaries, a harmless drudge'.

A

DICTIONARY

OF THE

ENGLISH LANGUAGE:

IN WHICH

The WORDS are deduced from their ORIGINALS,

AND

ILLUSTRATED in their DIFFERENT SIGNIFICATIONS

BY

EXAMPLES from the best WRITERS.

TO WHICH ARE PREFIXED,

A HISTORY of the LANGUAGE,

AND

AN ENGLISH GRAMMAR.

BY SAMUEL JOHNSON, A.M.

IN TWO VOLUMES.

VOL. I.

LONDON,
Printed by W. STRAHAN,
For J. and P. KNAPTON; T. and T. LONGMAN; C. HITCH and L. HAWES;
A. MILLAR; and R. and J. DODSLEY.
MDCCLV.

Joseph of Cupertino, Methodius of Olympus.

19 SEPTEMBER

In 1356, the Black Prince, son to Edward III, defeats the French again at Poitiers, capturing the French king, John II. The Black Prince demands such a huge ransom that it could not be paid so that the French king lives the rest of his life in England. John II is held for a time in the Savoy Palace, the site of the present-day Savoy Hotel, but finishes his life in the Tower of London.

On this day in 1911, William Golding is born in Cornwall. He will go on to win the Nobel Prize for Literature. By far his best-known novel is *Lord of the Flies*, a book about boys turning savage on a desert island.

 Emily de Rodat, Januarius, Theodore of Canterbury.

In 1854, the Battle of Alma is fought, with British and French forces against the Russians. Often considered the first major battle of the Crimean War, the more famous Battle of Balaclava, with the Charge of the Light Brigade and the Thin Red Line, comes later.

Eustace, Madelgaire, martyrs of Korea.

In 1327, Edward II is murdered in Berkeley Castle, after attempts to starve and poison him fail. The final method involves a red-hot poker being inserted where it doesn't show.

Also on this day, in 1866, the writer H. G. Wells is born in Kent. He will go on to produce classics of science fiction, often showing extraordinary insight into the future. His most famous works include *The Time Machine*, *The Invisible Man*, *War of the Worlds*, *The Shape of Things to Come* and *The Island of Dr Moreau*.

The feast day of Matthew, apostle and evangelist, writer of the first Gospel.

22 SEPTEMBER

In 1791, Michael Faraday, known as the 'Father of Electricity', is born in London. He will go on to discover electromagnetic induction and the laws of electrolysis. He is also the first to isolate benzene and to synthesise chlorocarbons.

 Phocas, Thomas of Villanueva, The Martyrs of Agaunum.

23 SEPTEMBER

In 1846, Neptune is discovered by German astronomer Johann Galle. Neptune is the eighth planet from the sun, with only Pluto outside it.

Adamnan, Linus, Thecla of Iconium.

In 1975, the southwest face of Everest is scaled for the first time by British climbers Dougal Haston and Douglas Scott.

 Gerard of Csanad.

In 1857, the relief of the first Siege of Lucknow during the Indian Mutiny by Sir Henry Havelock takes place. Havelock and his men also relieved the more famous siege of Cawnpore. His statue stands at the southeast corner of Trafalgar Square, London, one of those surrounding Nelson's Column.

 Cadoc, Finbarr, Francis of Camporosso, Sergius of Radonezh.

26 SEPTEMBER

In 1847, Shakespeare's birthplace on Henley Street in Stratford-upon-Avon is purchased by a body of trustees to be preserved for the nation.

 Colman of Lann Elo, Cyprian and Jutina, Nilus of Rossano.

27 SEPTEMBER

In 1066, William the Conqueror crosses the channel in his ship, the Mora, and lands a fleet at Pevensey, spending the night in an ancient Roman fort.

Elzear, Vincent de Paul.

28 SEPTEMBER

In 1745, around this date, the national anthem 'God Save the King' is sung for the first time in London theatres. The relevant king is George II.

29 SEPTEMBER

Michaelmas – Archangel Michael's feast day and traditionally the third English Quarter Day, when rents become due. Michael is the patron of artists, police officers, soldiers and grocers. He is a very martial angel indeed and carries a sword and a pair of scales to weigh souls.

This day is also the feast of the Archangel Gabriel, who brought a message to Mary. As a result, the angel is the patron saint of postmen. It used to be in March, but sometimes the post is delayed.

Finally, on this day in 1758, Horatio Nelson is born at Burnham Thorpe in Norfolk. He will go on to be quite successful as a Royal Navy Admiral.

Cyriacus the Recluse, Archangels Michael, Gabriel and Raphael.

30 SEPTEMBER

In 1938, Prime Minister Neville Chamberlain returns from a meeting with Adolf Hitler in Munich in which Hitler stated his desire not to go to war with Britain. Chamberlain waves the agreement in the air and declares it to represent 'peace in our time'. World War II breaks out less than a year later.

 Honorius of Canterbury, Otto of Bamberg. Also Jerome, who translated the Bible from Hebrew and Greek into Latin.

ODE TO AUTUMN

Season of mists and mellow fruitfulness!
Close bosom-friend of the maturing sun;
Conspiring with him how to load and bless
With fruit the vines that round the thatch-eaves run;
To bend with apples the mossed cottage-trees,
And fill all fruit with ripeness to the core;
To swell the gourd, and plump the hazel shells
With a sweet kernel; to set budding more,
And still more, later flowers for the bees,
Until they think warm days will never cease,
For Summer has o'erbrimmed their clammy cells.

Who hath not seen thee oft amid thy store?
Sometimes whoever seeks abroad may find
Thee sitting careless on a granary floor,
Thy hair soft-lifted by the winnowing wind;
Or on a half-reaped furrow sound asleep,
Drowsed with the fume of poppies, while thy hook
Spares the next swath and all its twined flowers;
And sometimes like a gleaner thou dost keep
Steady thy laden head across a brook;
Or by a cider-press, with patient look,
Thou watchest the last oozings, hours by hours.

Where are the songs of Spring? Ay, where are they?
Think not of them, thou hast thy music too, -
While barred clouds bloom the soft-dying day
And touch the stubble-plains with rosy hue;
Then in a wailful choir the small gnats mourn
Among the river sallows, borne aloft
Or sinking as the light wind lives or dies;
And full-grown lambs loud bleat from hilly bourn;
Hedge-crickets sing, and now with treble soft
The redbreast whistles from a garden-croft;
And gathering swallows twitter in the skies.

John Keats

AUTUMN

utumn is a season for crisp, cold nights and clear skies, though in England it does sometimes rain for much of it. It can be windy, so it's a time of year when kites can be made and flown, or bought if you must. Fogs and frost are common across the country, making it the season for warm coats, hot soup and curling up with a good book in the evenings. Trees shed their leaves in drifts of beautiful colours at this time.

Autumn lasts from the September equinox – around 22nd or 23rd – up to the winter solstice and longest night in December. The final crops are harvested at the beginning of October, so that the fields are bare except for birds readying themselves to migrate further south to warmer climes. Conkers are available from horse chestnut trees and the world conker championship takes place in Ashton, Northamptonshire on a Sunday around 14 October.

After that final harvest, you will find many fruits and vegetables in the shops at autumn, such as plums, damsons, pears, onions, aubergines and late-fruiting varieties of raspberries. Autumn is when many farmers slaughter animals, so it is also the best time for mutton, which is meat from sheep two or more years old. It is not quite as tender as lamb, but is excellent in pies and stews, braises and pot-roasts. Meat does not have to have preservatives in it if it is eaten fresh. It's worth the time to find a decent butcher as most supermarket meat in plastic contains preservatives to allow them to be displayed for longer. If fish is more to your taste, there are many at their best in autumn, such as mussels, crab, and wild sea-bass. Again, it's worth asking where the fish were caught and how long ago. The oyster season lasts until March though you want to eat them as fresh as possible. The last fresh British apples appear in the shops in autumn. If you can, try to find Worcester

apples, or Cox's Orange Pippins, as they are two absolutely delicious varieties and not at all common any more.

If you have found a farmer's market, autumn is a time to buy fruit jams. Home-made ones might have a soft white fuzz on the top that does you no harm and can be removed with a knife. If you keep them in the fridge, they'll last for months.

Feasts and festivals of autumn include: St Luke's Day on 18 October, Trafalgar Day on 21 October, St Crispin's Day and the anniversary of the Battle of Agincourt on 25 October, Hallowe'en on 31 October, Guy Fawkes Night on 5 November, Remembrance Sunday on 11 November and St Andrew's Day on 30 November.

The days grow shorter throughout autumn and the land hardens with cold, before winter arrives in December.

OCTOBER

October was the eighth month for the Romans and our tenth. The old English word for the month was 'Winmōnath', the wine month, when grapes were gathered for harvesting. As far north as Hadrian's Wall, grapes were once grown for wine-making. It seems an odd name for a British October, but between the ninth and fourteenth centuries, the world was a little warmer than it is today. Greenland, for example, was settled by Vikings in this period, but then abandoned in the fourteenth century when it became too cold to survive comfortably.

In the Hertfordshire town of Braughing, 2 October is known as Old Man's Day and the church bells are rung. This particular custom comes from the sixteenth century, where a pallbearer at the funeral of Matthew Wall stumbled with the coffin and jolted the occupant awake. When he recovered from the shock, Wall lived long enough to remarry. He died for the second time in 1595 and left money in his will that the church bells be rung each year in thanks for his escape. He also left a shilling for a poor man to be paid to sweep the church path. Today, the job is given to local children with brooms.

October is a cold, crisp month, with the trees losing their leaves in great drifts of ochre, russet and reds that children love to kick. The clocks go back an hour in this month, marking the beginning of the darker months. It ends, famously, with Hallowe'en, often considered a pagan festival, though it began as the night before All Saints, or 'All Hallows' on the first day of November, followed by All Souls on 2 November. Hallowe'en seems to have come about from the idea that the spirits are more active on the eve of All Hallows – or Hallowe'en. Like New Year's Day it has long been considered a time for divination. On Hallowe'en, a young girl is said to be able to read the name of her future husband in an unbroken apple-peel tossed over her shoulder. As Terry Pratchett pointed out, the girl was likely to be disappointed unless her future love was called 'Scscs'.

As customs go, there are few things more annoying than a group of small children dressed as vampires and witches turning up at your door to demand sweets while a parent waits nearby with the engine running. A bucket of water may be considered cruel by some, but these writers believe it to be a wonderful remedy to a difficult social situation.

TRADITIONAL CUSTOMS

Conker Championships

On the second Sunday of October, the World Conker championships are held in Ashton, near Corby in Northamptonshire. Children and adults can compete, but must use conkers provided, so there is no opportunity to bake or varnish them beforehand. Around three thousand people come to watch and it's a fun family day out.

Apple Day

Apple day on 21 October is a celebration of apples and cider around the country, from the south coast up to Yorkshire. Your County Council will be able to tell you if there is a local event near you.

Harvest Festivals

Many Harvest festivals take place around the country in late September and October. Most of these are for crops, but on the second Sunday of October, the 'Harvest of the Sea' service takes place at St Mary-at-Hill church in London, close by Billingsgate fish market. Fishing nets are hung in the church and a great decorative platter of fish is provided by the Billingsgate traders.

Pheasant Shooting

Pheasant shooting season begins in England, Scotland and Wales on 1 October, ending on 1 February. In England and Wales, the Woodcock season also opens on 1 October, ending on 31 January. In Scotland, the Woodcock season opens a month earlier on 1 September.

Punkie Night

The fourth Thursday in October is Punkie night for the people of Hinton St George in Somerset. Local children make home-made lanterns from mangolds, a kind of beet, hollowing them out and setting a candle inside. They proceed through the town with their lamps or 'punkies' collecting a few pence at each door. The tradition is believed to have started with the men of the village wandering over to nearby Chiselborough Fair for some heavy drinking. Legend has it the women of the village set lights in the Mangolds and came looking for their errant husbands.

Lion Sermon

On 16 October, an annual service is held at the church of St Katharine Cree on Leadenhall Street, London. It is to commemorate an extraordinary incident that befell one John Gayer, a 17th century Merchant. On his travels in Arabia, he became lost in the desert. Unarmed and alone, he came across a hunting lion and feared for his life. Recalling the biblical story of Daniel, he knelt and prayed for deliverance. When he opened his eyes, there were footprints all around, but the lion had gone. Gayer left a bequest to the poor of St Katharine's parish upon his death in 1649.

1 OCTOBER

Pheasant shooting season begins in England, Scotland and Wales, ending on 1 February. In England and Wales, the woodcock season also opens, ending on 31 January. In Scotland, the woodcock season opens a month earlier on 1 September.

On this day in 1908, the Model T Ford goes on sale. It is the first really affordable car and goes on to sell sixteen million. Henry Ford's production line is a pioneering example of mass production, introducing techniques that will revolutionise manufacturing in the twentieth century.

 Gregory the Enlightener, Nicetius of Trier, Romanus the Melodist, Theresa of Lisieux.

2 OCTOBER

In 1452, Richard III is born, the last English king to die on the battlefield as the Tudors came to power in the form of Henry VII. Richard's later reputation suffers through Tudor propaganda and the image of a cruel hunchback by William Shakespeare. His famous hunchback could have been no more than the mass of muscle that comes from fighting with a broadsword. At the battle of Bosworth Field, Richard refused to run, bellowing out these final words: 'I will die King of England'.

Feast of Guardian Angels, Leger. The St. Leger horse race is named after an eighteenth century Colonel St Leger, not the actual saint.

3 OCTOBER

In 1916, James Wight OBE is born in Sunderland, better known as 'James Herriot', his pen name. He will go on to write a number of humorous books based around his experiences as a vet. He is best known for *It Shouldn't Happen to a Vet* and *If Only They Could Talk*.

Gerard of Brogne, The Two Hewalds, Thomas of Hereford.

4 OCTOBER

In 1226, St Francis of Assisi dies. He is the founder of the Franciscan monastic order, and the patron saint of animals, merchants, Italy and ecologists.

On this day in 1957, the first space satellite, Sputnik 1, is launched by the Soviet Union. Along with the first probe to Venus, the first man and woman in space and the first moon probe, this is the beginning of a period of incredible achievement that forced America to catch up.

Francis.

5 OCTOBER

In 2006, the Siege of Nawzad ends in Iraq. Forty Gurkha soldiers defend a police station for ten days against 28 full-scale attacks and constant sniper and mortar fire by Taliban fighters. By the end, approximately 100 Taliban fighters have been killed and three Gurkhas wounded with no fatalities.

 Maurus, Placid.

6 OCTOBER

In 1769, Captain James Cook discovers New Zealand, amazing the Maoris with this claim. Decades of fighting follow as they argue about it.

Bruno.

In 1571, the Battle of Lepanto is fought – a spectacular victory against the Moslem Ottoman Empire fleet by Don John of Austria, leading a fleet of Papal forces. It is the last major battle to involve galleys, a form of sea warfare going back for many thousands of years. G. K. Chesterton wrote a superb poem about the battle, which begins: 'White founts falling in the courts of the sun…'

In 1908, *The Wind in the Willows* is published, written by Kenneth Grahame. It becomes a classic, introducing the world to Rat, Mole and the wonderful Mr Toad of Toad Hall.

Justina, Osyth.

Demetrius, Margaret, Palagia the Penitent, Sergius and Bacchus.

9 OCTOBER

Henry VI of England is restored to his throne by the Earl of Warwick, the man known as 'The Kingmaker'. Henry VI lost the French territory gained by his father Henry V, despite being crowned King of France as well as England. He is one of the worst kings of England in history, ranking right up there with Edward II. Like Edward, Henry is eventually murdered.

 Denis of Paris, Louis Bertrand, John Leonardi.

10 OCTOBER

In 1972, Sir John Betjeman becomes the poet laureate. His best-known works include 'A Subaltern's Love Song' and 'Slough'.

 Daniel and six Italian Friars, who were martyred in Morocco, Francis Borgia, Paulinus of York.

11 OCTOBER

In 1889, James Prescott Joule dies in Sale, near Manchester. During his life, he demonstrated that heat is a form of energy and his work became the basis for the theory of conservation of energy. With Lord Kelvin, he did groundbreaking work on temperatures and formulated the absolute scale. The unit of energy, 'joule', is named after him, just as the absolute-zero scale is named after Kelvin.

 Alexander Sauli, Bruno, Ethelburga of Barking.

12 OCTOBER

In 1537, the often forgotten son of Henry VIII and Jane Seymour, Edward VI, is born. He becomes king at the age of nine in 1547. Edward VI was physically frail and dies at the age of 15, probably from tuberculosis. Despite his extreme youth, he was an extremely able Latin scholar. His most important legacy was *The Book of Common Prayer*, written with Cranmer, the Archbishop of Canterbury.

 Serafino, Wilfred.

In 1943, Italy declares war on Germany, having seen which way the war is going.

Gerald of Aurillac. Also Edward the Confessor, King of England.

In 1066, William the Conqueror fights the Battle of Hastings, beating the exhausted soldiers of Harold after they had marched 200 miles in five days.

Also on this day in 1633, James II, son of Charles I, is born. He will inherit after his brother Charles II died. In a similar tale to King John losing the crown jewels in the Wash when he was surprised by a fast tide in 1216, James II manages to drop the Great Seal of England in the Thames in 1688.

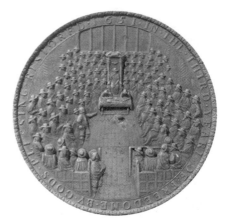

Pope Callistus I, Justus of Lyons.

15 OCTOBER

In 1881, P. G. Wodehouse (Pelham Grenville) is born in Guildford. The creator of Jeeves and Bertie Wooster, Psmith and Ukridge, he is the author of more than ninety books and one of the great comic writers of the twentieth century.

On this day in 1997, Andy Green in *Thrust* SSC is the first man to beat the speed of sound in a car, reaching a speed of 763 miles per hour at Black Rock Desert, USA.

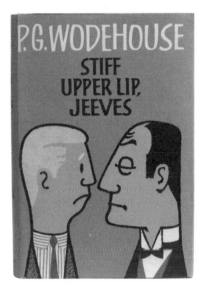

 Teresa of Avila, Thecla of Kitzingen.

16 OCTOBER

In 1815, Napoleon arrives at St Helena, after losing the Battle of Waterloo. He will spend the rest of his life on this remote British island in the Atlantic, off the west coast of Africa.

 Gerard Majella, Hedwig, Margaret Mary, Marguerite d'Youville.

17 OCTOBER

In 1930, France announces the creation of the Maginot Line, a solid defence of concrete and machine-gun positions against future German invasion. Unfortunately, the Germans go round it by invading Belgium first.

Ethelbert and Ethelred of Kent, who were martyred together. Also, Ignatius of Antioch.

18 OCTOBER

In 1860, British troops destroy the Emperor's Summer Palace in Peking (Beijing), China.

On this day in 1887, Russia sells Alaska to the US for seven million dollars. They see it as a frozen, worthless wilderness. Later, oil is found.

Justus of Beauvais. Also the feast day of the evangelist, friend of Paul and Gospel writer, Luke.

19 OCTOBER

In 202 BC, the Battle of Zama is fought around this date, the final battle of the second Punic War between Carthage and Rome. After the failure of the original Roman generals, command fell to Publius Cornelius Scipio, better known as 'Scipio Africanus'. His military genius turned the tide of the war and helped to preserve a Rome that would produce the Caesars and an empire only a century later. At Zama, Scipio used a mobile formation that could open up to let Hannibal's war elephants trundle straight through. The tactic worked beautifully, neutralising the threat and one of Hannibal's chief advantages. In the end, it came down to quality of the fighting men involved, and though the Romans were outnumbered, Scipio had the best Rome could produce. Hannibal was broken and forced to sue for peace, after more than twenty years of war.

 Frideswide, John of Rila, Peter of Alcántara.

20 OCTOBER

In 1714, George I is crowned in Westminster Abbey – the first of the Hanoverian kings. In 1701, the Act of Settlement forbade any future Catholic monarch. When Queen Anne died without heirs in August 1714, the Protestant Hanoverians come to the throne despite George hardly even speaking the language. His wife Sophia is a granddaughter of James I. It is a turbulent period, with the Scots supporting Jacobite Catholic rebellions in 1715 and again in 1745.

 Andrew of Crete, Bertilla Boscardin.

21 OCTOBER

Trafalgar Day, celebrated primarily in Portsmouth, Plymouth, Gosport and Greenwich.

On this day in 1772, Samuel Taylor Coleridge is born in Devonshire. A friend to William Wordsworth, he is best known for his poems 'Kubla Khan' and 'The Rime of the Ancient Mariner'.

> *In Xanadu did Kubla Khan*
> *A stately pleasure-dome*
> *   decree:*
> *Where Alph, the sacred river,*
> *   ran*
> *Through caverns measureless*
> *   to man*
> *Down to a sunless sea.*
>   **Extract from 'Kubla Khan'**
>   **by Coleridge**

 Fintan of Taghmon, Hilarion, John of Bridlington, Ursula and the Virgins.

22 OCTOBER

In 1962, the Cuban Missile Crisis develops. President Kennedy announces the discovery of Soviet missile sites in Cuba. He demands publicly that they be removed, and for six days the world totters on the brink of nuclear war. The Soviet leader, Nikita Kruschev, blinks first and agrees to remove the missiles.

 Donatus of Friesole, Philip of Heraclea.

23 OCTOBER

In 1942, the second battle of El Alamein takes place in Egypt, where Axis powers are forced to retreat. After three vicious years of war, this is a crucial victory and boost to morale. Famously, Churchill describes it as 'Not the beginning of the end, but, perhaps, the end of the beginning.'

On this day in 1921, John Boyd Dunlop dies, aged 81. He was the inventor of the pneumatic rubber tyre – and also the word 'pneumatic'. The Dunlop company still makes car tyres today.

Ignatius of Constantinople, John of Capistrano, Romanus of Rouen.

24 OCTOBER

In 1945, the execution of the Norwegian traitor Vidkun Quisling takes place. Quisling had collaborated openly with the Nazis. The word 'Quisling' is still used to mean traitor.

 Antony Mary Claret, Felix of Thibiuca.

25 OCTOBER

St Crispin's Day and the anniversary of the Battle of Agincourt. On this day in 1415, up to 25,000 French face 5,000 English. The French knights discover that 40,000 English longbow arrows fired every minute are a destructive force greater than any the world has ever seen. The practice of sticking two fingers up as an insult comes from this battle. When the French caught an English archer, they cut his bow-fingers off. The gesture came from the English archers, showing the French that they still had their fingers.

Chrysanthus and Daria, Crispin and Crispinian, Gaudentius of Brescia, John of Beverley, The Forty Martyrs of England and Wales.

26 OCTOBER

Close to or on this day in 899 AD, Alfred the Great dies. He is buried in Newminster Abbey, Winchester. The only king to have the title 'Great', Alfred beat the Danes, helped to unify England and began the navy.

On this day in 1881, the Gunfight at the OK Corral takes place in Tombstone, Arizona. It is perhaps the most famous gunfight in the history of the Wild West. Marshal Virgil Earp, his brothers Wyatt and Morgan and Doc Holliday, shoot it out with Frank McLaury, Tom McLaury, Ike Clanton, Billy Clanton and Billy Claibourne. Around thirty shots are fired in as many seconds. Both the McLaurys and Billy Clanton are killed. Virgil and Morgan Earp are later shot in revenge, though Virgil survives without the use of his right arm. Wyatt Earp comes through unscathed.

 Evaristus, Cedd.

27 OCTOBER

In 1914, Dylan Thomas, the Welsh poet and playwright, is born. He is most famous for his play *Under Milk Wood* and the poem 'Do not go gentle into that good night'.

Also on this day, in 939 AD, Athelstan, the first king of England, dies. He is buried in Malmesbury Abbey.

 Frumentius.

28 OCTOBER

In 1636, Harvard University is founded with a bequest from John Harvard, an English-born Puritan and the son of a butcher. It is the oldest university in America.

Also on this day, in 1942, an SS directive orders that children's mittens and socks should be sent from the death camps in Poland to SS families. An event such as the Holocaust should never be forgotten.

Demetrius of Rostov, Jude and Simon.

29 OCTOBER

In 1929, the Wall Street Crash takes place. Investors panic, selling shares. The US stock market collapses, bringing in a decade of mass unemployment and poverty for millions.

Colman of Kidmacduagh.

30 OCTOBER

In 1683, George II is born to his parents George I and Sophia. Like his father, he is born in Hanover and remains more German than English throughout his reign. George II's heir, Frederick, dies when he is hit in the eye by a tennis ball. Frederick's son George III is born in England, but is barking mad and manages to lose the American colonies as well.

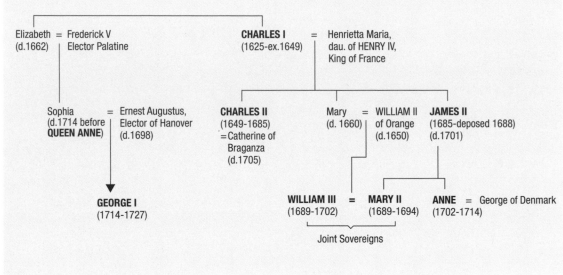

Alphonsus Rodriguez, Marcellus the Centurion.

31 OCTOBER

Hallowe'en, or All Hallows Eve. In ancient times, the evening of the first of November was Samhain, one of the great fire festivals.

Also on this day, in 1795, John Keats is born in London. 'Beauty is truth, truth Beauty.' Part of the Romantic movement in poetry, he remains one of the great English poets.

 Foillan, Wolfgang.

NOVEMBER

The ninth month for the Romans and our eleventh. The days grow shorter as they head to the winter solstice that falls around 21 December. For the Celts, the first of November was the feast of Samhain and the first day of winter and the year.

The month begins with the Church festivals of All Saints and All Souls. On All Souls, Catholics believe that reciting six 'Our Fathers', six 'Hail Marys' and six 'Glory be to the Fathers' will free a single soul from Purgatory into Heaven.

On the first Sunday in November, the London to Brighton Car Run takes place, open only to cars built before 1905. Between 300 and 600 vehicles take part each year, leaving Hyde Park in London at between seven and eight in the morning and ending up at the finish line on Madeira Drive in Brighton later the same day.

On 5 November, English children cheerfully celebrate the torture and execution of the Catholic Guy Fawkes, who tried to blow up the Houses of Parliament in 1605. The custom of making a 'Guy' by stuffing old clothes with newspapers to make a man is still fairly common around the country. The Guy can then be taken out on a go-cart or a pram and passing strangers are asked to contribute a 'penny for the guy.' This night is also known as 'Bonfire Night' and open-air events often involve a Guy being burned on a great fire. Guy Fawkes was actually hanged, drawn and quartered, which is harder to re-enact and frightens the children a bit.

Remembrance Day takes place on 11 November, commemorating those Britons who have died in wars, giving their lives for the peace and freedom of those they left behind. Services are held around the country on Remembrance Sunday, the closest Sunday to the eleventh. A two-minute silence is held nationally at 11 a.m. on Remembrance Sunday and also on the 11 November if it falls on another day. In the weeks before Remembrance Sunday, red poppies are sold everywhere by the British Legion, a tradition going back to 1921. The poppies are made in one place by ex-servicemen and women, where 70 per cent of the workers are disabled or suffer from chronic illness. The money raised goes to help the widows and orphans of those soldiers as well as the survivors.

Only one year has passed since World War II without a Briton dying on active service. That year was 1968. It is difficult to imagine a donation to charity that is better used or more deserved.

Winter deepens as November turns to December. The roads ice over and car windscreens have to be scraped or sprayed with de-icer. Snow is rarely seen in the south of England, though common in parts of the north and in Scotland.

November is a dark month in many ways. The Anglo-Saxon name for it was 'Blōtmōnath', the 'blood month', where farmed livestock would be slaughtered. It was also the month when fishermen beached their boats and settled in for a long winter before going out again in spring.

TRADITIONAL CUSTOMS

Devil's Stone, Devon

At the village of Shebbear in Devon, a large boulder lies, weighing around a ton. It is known as the Devil's Stone or the 'Shebbear Stone'. No one knows how the tradition started, but every 5 November local bell-ringers gather to ring the church bells, then break off, rush out and turn the stone right over.

On 10 November, the Lord Mayor of London makes his way in procession through London to the law courts to declare his loyalty to the crown. This is in accordance with King John's Charter to the city in 1215. The mayor travels in a gilded coach and pikemen and military bands take part. Half a million people come to watch the spectacle. It is also televised and remains a key event in London's calendar.

Tar Barrel-Rolling

The 5 of November sees the popular local event of Tar Barrels in the East Devon town of Ottery St Mary, birthplace of Samuel Taylor Coleridge. The whole day is set aside for the ancient tradition of carrying flaming barrels through the town. The barrels are prepared a year before and coated in tar before being soaked in paraffin and set alight. They are then carried flaming through the crowded streets, delighting huge crowds. Youngsters are the first to start the festivities with miniature barrels in the afternoon, but the barrels get progressively bigger until the final barrel, a vast hogshead, is set alight at midnight by the men in the market square to a roar from onlookers. Space is at a premium and so the sight of a flaming barrel careering towards you is not uncommon and genuinely quite frightening.

Carnival, Somerset

On the first Friday in November, Bridgwater in Somerset hosts the largest illuminated carnival in the world. The carnival involves enormous, decorated floats lit with thousands of bulbs, fireworks and around 150,000 visitors. It has been going since 1881 in this form. Earlier versions have their origins in Bonfire Night. In fact, the procession is always led by a float containing Guy Fawkes and his barrels of gunpowder.

Silent Change, London

On the second Friday in November, the 'Silent Change' takes place. After being elected at Michaelmas Day (29 September), the new Lord Mayor of London is sworn in, accepting the symbols of the office: a sword, a mace, a sceptre, an official seal and the City Purse. The change from old to new takes place in silence, hence the name. The Lord Mayor is head of the Corporation of London, Admiral of the Port of London, Chief Magistrate of the City and Chancellor of City University. To be elected, he must be a city Alderman and have served as a Sheriff. One of the oldest positions of authority anywhere, the office began in 1192. It is not to be confused with the Mayor of London, a job for which no qualifications are necessary.

1 NOVEMBER

All Saints or All Hallows Day. On this day in 1959, Britain's first motorway, the M1, officially opens. It has no speed limit until one of 70 mph is introduced in 1965. Cars like the E-Type Jaguar were capable of doing almost 150 mph along it until that time.

 All Saints, Benignus.

2 NOVEMBER

In 2003, the explorer Ranulph Fiennes and Dr Mike Stroud complete the last of seven marathons in seven days on seven continents. It is particularly remarkable considering that Fiennes is 59 years old and had previously undergone double heart bypass surgery.

 All Souls, Malachi, Justus of Trieste.

3 NOVEMBER

In 1957, the USSR launches the *Sputnik 2* space mission, carrying the first dog in space, Laika. She does not survive the trip.

Hubert, Malachy, Winifred.

4 NOVEMBER

In 1918, Wilfred Owen dies. He is perhaps the best-known poet of World War I. Owen had been sent home to a war hospital in Edinburgh, suffering from shell-shock. There he met fellow poet Siegfried Sassoon who was recuperating from a head wound. Sassoon told Owen he would 'stab him in the leg' if he tried to return to France, but Owen felt it was his duty. Only seven days before peace is declared, he is shot as he crosses a canal. His most famous poem is 'Dulce et Decorum Est'.

> *Gas! Gas! Quick, boys! – An*
> *   ecstasy of fumbling,*
> *Fitting the clumsy helmets*
> *   just in time;*
> *But someone still was yelling*
> *   out and stumbling,*
> *And flound'ring like a man in*
> *   fire or lime -*
> *Dim, through the misty panes*
> *   and thick green light,*
> *As under a green sea, I saw*
> *   him drowning.*
> *In all my dreams, before my*
> *   helpless sight,*
> *He plunges at me, guttering,*
> *   choking, drowning.*
>
> **Extract from 'Dulce et**
> **Decorum Est' by Wilfred Owen**

Charles Borromeo, Emeric.

5 NOVEMBER

In 1605, the Gunpowder Plot is discovered and Guy Fawkes is arrested for trying to assassinate the king and blow up the Houses of Parliament. He is cruelly tortured and executed with the other conspirators the following January. Bonfires and firework displays are held each year for small children to delight in what happened to him.

GUY FAWKES DAY.

Please to remember the Fifth of November,
The Gunpowder treason plot,
I see no reason why Gunpowder treason
Should ever be forgot.
A stick and a stake for Victoria's sake.
Hollo, boys! Hollo, boys!
God save the Queen

Zachariah and Elizabeth, the parents of John the Baptist.

6 NOVEMBER

In 1935, Britain's first single-wing fighter plane, the Hawker Hurricane, makes her maiden flight. Not quite as fast as the Supermarine Spitfire, Hurricanes could still reach 300 mph and have a smaller turning radius. The plane plays a vital role throughout World War II. Douglas Bader flew one in the Battle of Britain.

 Leonard, Winnoc.

7 NOVEMBER

In 1996, the Mars Global Surveyor is launched by NASA. It travels 466 million miles to reach Mars on 11 September 1997. The MGS cannot come back, but as you read this it is orbiting Mars every two hours, sending a complete record of the planetary surface in more detail than ever before.

Also on this day, in 2002, 98.97 per cent of Gibraltar residents vote not to share British sovereignty with Spain.

 Engelbert, Willibrord.

8 NOVEMBER

In 1656, Edmond Halley is born in London. He will go on to study the solar system and correctly predict the existence of the comet that is named after him. His prediction was not proven until 1758 after his death, when Halley's Comet returned.

 Godfrey of Amiens, Willehad. The Four Crowned Martyrs.

9 NOVEMBER

In 1841, Edward VII, son of Queen Victoria and her consort Albert, is born at Buckingham Palace. He is the first Emperor of India. His reign is later known as the Edwardian Period, 1901 to 1910. He is buried at St George's Chapel, Windsor.

Nectarius Kephalas, Theodore the Recruit.

10 NOVEMBER

In 1871, American journalist Henry Stanley is sent to Africa by his newspaper to find the lost Scottish missionary Dr David Livingstone. On this day, Stanley finally finds the man and famously says, 'Doctor Livingstone, I presume?'

 Andrew Avellino, Justus of Canterbury, Pope Leo the Great.

11 NOVEMBER

St Martin's Day or 'Martinmas'. Originally a Roman soldier, Saint Martin converted to Christianity and refused to fight, later becoming a monk, then a bishop in Gaul. Traditionally, it is also the last Scottish Quarter Day, when rents become due and all manner of official business is conducted.

Two days before 11 November 1920, four unidentified British bodies are taken from the WW1 battlefields of the Aisne, the Somme, Ypres and Arras. A blindfolded officer chooses one and the other three are reburied. The last is brought home and buried in the tomb of the Unknown Warrior on 11 November in Westminster Abbey with an honour guard of one hundred St George Cross veterans.

The coffin is made from English oak under a layer of French soil and a tablet of Belgian marble, representing the allies in the Great War. The letters of the inscription are formed from brass shell cases fired in that conflict. It reads: 'They buried him among the kings, because he had done good toward God and toward his house' – words based on Old Testament lines in the Book of Chronicles.

WW1 ends on 11 November 1918. Since that day, a two minute silence is held at 11 AM on the 11th day of the 11th month. On the closest Sunday, a further silence is held and members of the government and opposition lay wreaths at the Cenotaph in London in memory of the British dead in all wars.

Bartholomew of Grottaferrata, Martin of Tours, Theodore the Studite.

12 NOVEMBER

In 1944, after ten failed attacks by the RAF, it is no surprise that the Germans regarded their super-battleship *Tirpitz* as unsinkable. However, on this day, Lancaster bombers sank it.

Lebuin, Josaphat of Polotsk, Nilus of Ancyra.

13 NOVEMBER

In 1312, Edward III, son to Edward II and grandson to Edward I, is born. He will go on to be one of the most successful kings in English history. He was there for the start of the Hundred Years' War and won the naval battle of Sluys as well as the more famous Crécy in 1346. He becomes King of France as well, in 1340, and his successors keep Calais until it was lost by Mary I's Spanish husband in 1558.

Frances Cabrini, Homobonus, Pope Nicholas I, Stanislas Kostka.

14 NOVEMBER

In 1940, the bombing of Coventry takes place. After breakthroughs decrypting the German Enigma code machine, Churchill had advance warning of the attack and could have evacuated the city. If he had done so, he would have revealed that the Allies had broken the code. Churchill made a bitterly hard decision and did not warn the city. Up to a thousand people died and Coventry was all but destroyed. The Germans remained unaware that their Enigma code had been cracked until the end of the war. Many more lives were saved as a result, but it is still one of those times when few people would have liked to be in Churchill's shoes, faced with that decision.

 Dyfrig, Gregory Palamas, Lawrence O'Toole.

15 NOVEMBER

In 1996, the Stone of Scone, or 'Stone of Destiny' is returned to Scotland, having been taken from them by Edward I in the thirteenth century. A vital part of the coronation of Scottish kings, its lack meant that Robert the Bruce had to be crowned without it. Ever since then, it has been part of the coronation chair in Westminster Abbey. The last monarch to have been crowned sitting on it was Elizabeth II in 1953. Although it is now in Edinburgh castle, arrangements are in place to return it for any future British coronations.

CHURCHMAN'S CIGARETTES

Albert the Great, the theologian who taught St. Thomas Aquinas. Also, Fintan of Rheinau, Leopold of Austria.

16 NOVEMBER

In 1965, Soviet unmanned reconnaissance probe *Venera 3* is launched at Venus. It crash-lands on 1 March 1966, becoming the first human artefact to reach another planet.

Edmund of Abingdon, Eucherius of Lyons, Gertrude of Helfta, Margaret of Scotland.

17 NOVEMBER

In 1558, Elizabeth I ascends the throne, becoming Queen of England and Ireland.

On this day in 1604, one of Elizabeth I's favourites, Sir Walter Ralegh, is tried for treason and imprisoned in the Tower of London.

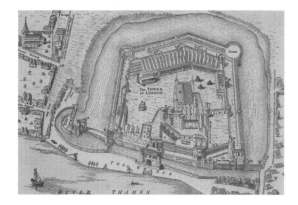

Dionysus of Alexandria, Elizabeth of Hungary, Gregory the Wonderworker, Gregory of Tours, Hugh of Lincoln.

18 NOVEMBER

On this day in 1852, the state funeral of Arthur Wellesley, first Duke of Wellington takes place at St Paul's Cathedral in London. The interior of the cathedral is covered in black velvet for the occasion and illuminated by gaslight. The gun carriage and coffin of Cornish porphyry weigh seventeen and a half tons and are drawn by bay horses sporting black ostrich plumes. The procession makes its way from Chelsea Royal Hospital to the bottom of Ludgate Hill. At this point, the horses are exhausted by the tremendous weight. Men of the Royal Navy step forward to take their place and, with ropes, pull the sarcophagus and carriage up the hill to St Paul's. This becomes the tradition for full state funerals and is re-enacted for Sir Winston Churchill's funeral in 1965.

Also on this day in 1901, Britain and America agree to build a canal across the Isthmus of Panama after a failed French attempt. The Panama Canal becomes one of the wonders of the modern world. President Theodore Roosevelt tells his contractors to 'Make the dirt fly!'

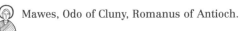 Mawes, Odo of Cluny, Romanus of Antioch.

19 NOVEMBER

In 1600, Charles I, King of Great Britain and Ireland, is born. He enters into a struggle against parliamentary power and rules without them for eleven years. The Royalists (Cavaliers) and Parliamentarians (Roundheads) fight the English Civil War, which Charles loses. He is executed on 30 January 1649. Attempts to rule without a king eventually fail after Oliver Cromwell's death and Charles I's son is invited to take the throne in 1660 – known as 'The Restoration'. Unfortunately for the succession, Charles II has three stillborn legitimate children and almost twenty illegitimate ones. Another of his father's sons inherits the throne on his death – James II.

On this day in 1863, Lincoln delivers the Gettysburg Address, beginning: 'Four score and seven years ago, our father brought forth on this continent a new nation, conceived in liberty and dedicated to the proposition that all men are created equal.'

Alphonsus Rodriguez, Barlaam of Antioch, John del Castillo, Mechtilde of Helfta.

20 NOVEMBER

In 1947, Princess Elizabeth marries Lieutenant Philip Mountbatten at Westminster Abbey. Elizabeth is crowned six years later. Since becoming queen, she has made more than 250 overseas visits, including 23 to Canada. She celebrated her Golden Jubilee as queen in 2003. More than a million people filled the roads around Buckingham Palace in London to see her appear on the balcony.

Bernward, Edmund, Felix of Valois.

21 NOVEMBER

In 1953, the 'Piltdown man' skull is revealed as a hoax. At first, the skull was believed to be the 'missing link' in evolution, proving a connection between mankind and apes, as had been theorised. 'Discovered' in 1911, the skull was put together using the jawbone of an orang-utan. The best suspect for the identity of the hoaxer is Charles Dawson, who found the skull. However, no one ever admitted to it.

 Pope Gelasius I.

22 NOVEMBER

In 1963, John F. Kennedy, the thirty-fifth President of the United States, is killed in Dallas, Texas. Lee Harvey Oswald is named as his killer, though there are many conspiracy theories even to this day.

Cecilia, patron of musicians.

23 NOVEMBER

In 1852, around this date, the first red post boxes, or pillar boxes, are introduced in the Channel Islands. The idea for them came from the novelist Anthony Trollope, who worked for the Post Office at that time. They are installed on the mainland in 1853.

Alexander Nevsky, Columban, Felicity.

24 NOVEMBER

In 1916, Sir Hiram Maxim, a US-born British inventor, dies. His most famous invention is certainly the first fully automatic machine gun, used by both sides in World War I. He also invented the 'Captive Flying Machine' fairground ride, with small carriages attached to poles that whip round and give the illusion of flying. There is still one 1904 original in operation at Blackpool Pleasure Beach.

Chrysogonus, Colman of Cloyne, Flora and Mary, The Martyrs of Vietnam. Also the writer and theologian John of the Cross.

In 1952, Agatha Christie's most famous murder mystery, *The Mousetrap*, opens at the Ambassador theatre in London. It has never closed and is the world's longest running play. You'll have to see it to find out the identity of the murderer.

In 1922, Howard Carter and Lord Carnarvon finally open the tomb of King Tutankhamun in the Valley of Kings, Egypt. It is a slow, painstaking process and it is months before they lay eyes on the inner tomb, containing the famous gold sarcophagus of the young pharoah and many other items of incredible value and antiquity.

 Catherine of Alexandria. Also, Mercury, a Roman soldier.

John Berchmans, Leonard of Port Maurice, Peter of Alexandria.

27 NOVEMBER

In 1582, William Shakespeare marries Anne Hathaway by special license. He is eighteen. She is twenty-six and pregnant. They will have three children together. He goes on to become the most famous playwright of any age. His best works include *Macbeth*, *Henry V*, *Romeo and Juliet*, *King Lear*, *Hamlet* – too many to list. He is also the author of hundreds of sonnets. Perhaps the best known of them begins: 'Shall I compare thee to a summer's day?'

On this day in 1701, Anders Celsius is born, a Swedish astronomer. He is best known for the creation of the Celsius temperature scale, which sets the melting point of ice at zero degrees and the boiling point of water at 100 degrees. It is also known as 'Centigrade' – meaning a scale of a hundred degrees. Alternatively, temperature can be measured in Kelvin, from absolute zero, or Fahrenheit, which used human body temperature as the 100-degree mark. Lack of accurate testing meant that human body temperature is actually 98.4 degrees on the Fahrenheit scale.

Also on this day in 1966, actor and raconteur Clive Room is born in London.

 Gregory of Sinai, Virgil of Salzburg.

In 1757, the poet, artist, visionary and genius William Blake is born in London. He is perhaps most famous for writing 'Jerusalem', which begins, 'And did those feet in ancient times…' and 'The Tyger', which is about a tiger.

In 939 AD, Edmund I, 'The Magnificent', a Saxon king, is crowned at Kingston-upon-Thames. The second king of all England after Athelstan, he defeated the Norse King of York, Olaf Guthfrithson and the Britons of Strathclyde, which he turned over to the King of the Scots. He is buried in Glastonbury Abbey.

 James of the March, Catherine Labouré, Stephen the Younger.

Sernin.

30 NOVEMBER

St Andrew's Day, the Scottish Patron Saint. On this day in 1016, King Canute (sometimes written Cnut) ascends the throne of England.

Also on this day, in 1874, Winston Churchill is born six weeks prematurely in the cloakroom of Blenheim Palace, his ancestral home.

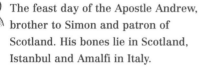 The feast day of the Apostle Andrew, brother to Simon and patron of Scotland. His bones lie in Scotland, Istanbul and Amalfi in Italy.

DECEMBER

The last cold breath of the year. Named for the Romans' tenth month before they added January and February. It is strange that no one ever changed the name to something like 'Duodecember', for twelfth month, but it's probably too late now.

There are literally hundreds of ancient customs around the country that find their centre in Christmas. In Dorset and Somerset, the Burning of the Ashen Faggot – a bundle of sticks – was once more popular, but still survives in places. The Faggot in question is a log of Ash wrapped around with smaller branches. Burning merrily, it is the centrepiece of drinking and celebration on Christmas Eve. In other places, the same idea is seen in the Yule log. In that version, a small piece of the log is saved to be burned with the new log next year, lending a sense of continuity to the passing years.

One lovely old belief, similar to the sun dancing on Easter morning, is that cattle in their stalls will kneel at midnight on Christmas Eve, in honour of the occasion.

Since 1918, King's College Chapel in Cambridge has held a service on Christmas Eve, open to anyone willing to queue all day. It is worth doing once in your life as the setting is perfect and the congregation sing all the old favourite carols, usually ending with 'Hark the Herald Angels'. The high notes of that one are a shade too high for one of the writers, prompting his sudden descent into bass, from which there is often no return. You will need to arrive long before nine in the morning, to be admitted around 1.30 in the afternoon.

After the presents, the carols, the cards, the turkey and the Queen's speech on Christmas Day, the year draws to a close on 31 December, or New Year's Eve. Many thousands gather in Trafalgar Square to welcome the New Year, or Hogmanay as it is known in Scotland, Northumberland, Cumberland, Westmoreland and Yorkshire. Elsewhere, friends and family gather in homes or at parties to see the year off with a bang. In the end is the beginning; in the old is the new – and the year begins again.

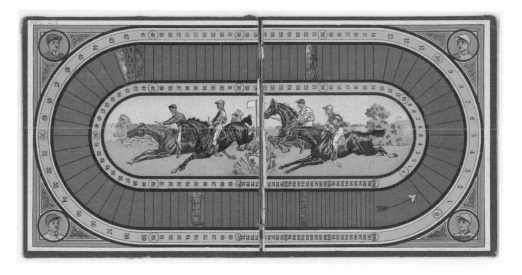

1 DECEMBER

In 1990, French and British engineers meet in the middle of the Channel Tunnel for the first time. At 31 miles long, the tunnel is considered to be one of the wonders of the modern world.

Eligius, Natalia.

2 DECEMBER

In 1697, the first service is held in St Paul's Cathedral, rebuilt by Christopher Wren after the Great Fire of London. Famous tombs in the building include those of Nelson, Wellington, Lord Kitchener, Florence Nightingale, T. E. Lawrence, Sir Alexander Fleming, Gordon of Khartoum, Wren himself and many others.

Viviana.

3 DECEMBER

In 1967, the first successful heart transplant is performed by Christiaan Barnard in Cape Town, South Africa. The recipient, Louis Washkansky, lives for only eighteen days after the operation.

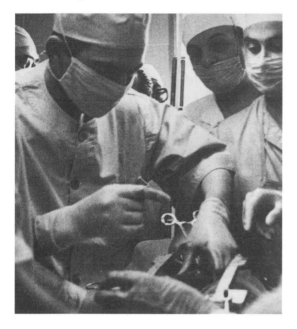

 Cassian of Tangier, Francis Xavier, Lucius.

4 DECEMBER

In 1829, the Abolition of Suttee by Lord William Bentinck is announced in India. Suttee was the practice of putting live widows on the funeral pyres of their husbands. It was banned previously in 1798, but it was difficult to stamp out – no pun intended. The British ban was only partly successful as the practice still goes on today in remote rural areas of India.

Barbara, John of Damascus, Osmund.

5 DECEMBER

In 1872, the Mary Celeste is found adrift, one of the great mysteries of history. Having sailed from New York on 7 November of that year, the ship was found without a soul aboard. There is some evidence of the crew leaving in a great hurry, abandoning their pipes and boots. Sir Arthur Conan Doyle would later explore the mystery in a short story, bringing it to popular attention.

 Birinus, Nicetius of Trier Sabas.

6 DECEMBER

In 1877, the world's first recording of a human voice is heard. The inventor of the 'Phonograph', Thomas Edison, records himself reciting 'Mary had a little lamb' and plays it back.

Abraham of Kratia. Also St. Nicholas, best known as Santa Niclaus, or Santa Claus.

7 DECEMBER

In 1941, the Japanese attack on Pearl Harbor takes place. Pearl Harbor is situated on Oahu Island in the Pacific, midway between Japan and the US. The event brings the US into World War II.

Ambrose.

8 DECEMBER

In 1980, John Lennon dies in New York, having been shot by a fan. His murderer, Mark Chapman, is still in prison. Chapman carried a copy of *Catcher in the Rye*, which has become part of the mythology around that book. In any survey of reading habits of psychopathic killers, *Catcher in the Rye* always tops the list.

As with any great artist, the personal tragedy is only part of the loss. Though Lennon's relationship with Paul McCartney was occasionally rocky, they were beginning to be reconciled. There is a good chance they would have resumed the greatest music-writing partnership of the twentieth century.

The feast of the Immaculate Conception. Also, Budoc, Romaric.

9 DECEMBER

In 1608, John Milton is born, author of the epic poems 'Paradise Lost' and 'Paradise Regained'. The old joke goes that he wrote 'Paradise Lost' when he married, then wrote 'Paradise Regained' when his wife died.

> *Here at least, we may be free;*
> *the almighty hath not built*
> *Here for his envy, will not*
> *drive us hence:*
> *Here we may reign secure,*
> *and in my choice*
> *To reign is worth ambition*
> *though in Hell:*
> *Better to reign in Hell than*
> *serve in Heav'n*
> **Paradise Lost**, Book 1

 Hipparchus and Philotheus, Peter Fourier.

10 DECEMBER

In 1907, Rudyard Kipling becomes the first British author to be awarded the then new Nobel Prize for Literature. A superb writer of prose and poetry, Kipling is best known for the prose *Jungle Book* and the poem 'If'.

Eulalia, Miltiades

11 DECEMBER

In 1936, Edward VIII abdicates. Part of his speech is drafted by Winston Churchill. His brother George VI – the father of Elizabeth II – becomes king. George VI is a shy man with a stammer and had never expected to become king. He rules throughout World War II, refusing to leave London during the Blitz. He dies in 1952 and is buried in St George's Chapel, Windsor.

 Pope Damasus I, Daniel the Stylite.

12 DECEMBER

In 1804, Spain declares war on Britain, having been persuaded by Napoleon to join France.

Edburga of Minster, Finnian of Clonard, Jane Frances de Chantal.

13 DECEMBER

In 1577, Sir Francis Drake sets sail from Plymouth and is away for three years. He endures storms and mutiny, but plunders Spanish treasure ships and returns with a fortune. He is knighted in Plymouth on the deck of his ship, the *Golden Hind*, by Elizabeth I.

Lucy, Odilia.

14 DECEMBER

In 1895, George VI, son of George V and father to Queen Elizabeth II, is born at Sandringham in Norfolk. A younger son, he did not expect to inherit and would not have if his older brother Edward had not abdicated.

On this day in 1972, the final Apollo mission, *Apollo 17*, leaves the surface of the moon. Before taking off, the astronauts unveil a plaque that reads: 'Here man completed his first exploration of the Moon, December 1972 AD. May the spirit of peace in which we came be reflected in the lives of all mankind.'

Spiridion, Venantius Fortunatus.

15 DECEMBER

In 1965, the *Gemini 6* manned space mission makes rendezvous with *Gemini 7*, staying in close proximity during an entire orbit.

 Mary di Rosa, Nino.

16 DECEMBER

In 1775, Jane Austen is born, the writer of spectacularly dull novels beloved of women everywhere. Author of *Northanger Abbey*, *Pride and Prejudice*, *Emma*, *Mansfield Park*, *Sense and Sensibility* and *Persuasion*. *Emma* is probably the worst of them.

 Adelaide.

The ancient Roman festival of Saturnalia begins, lasting six days.

On this day in 1778, Sir Humphry Davy is born in Cornwall. He will go on to discover the anaesthetic properties of laughing gas, and the elements potassium, sodium, barium, strontium, magnesium and calcium. He is most famous for devising safety lamps for use in mining.

Also on this day in 1857, Sir Francis Beaufort dies in Sussex. His scale to measure wind force, the Beaufort scale, is still in use today.

In 1856, Sir Joseph John Thomson is born near Manchester. He will go on to discover the existence of the electron. He also pioneered mass spectrometry and discovered the existence of isotopes of elements. He wins the Nobel Prize for Physics in 1906.

 Winebald.

 Begga, Olympias, Sturm.

19 DECEMBER

In 1851, J. M. W. Turner dies, one of the great English painters. He is most famous for paintings like *The Fighting Temeraire* and *The Battle of Trafalgar*, as well as landscapes. He is particularly good with storms, fire and sunsets and any exhibition of his work is always worth a look.

 Nemesion.

20 DECEMBER

In 1803, France turns New Orleans over to the United States as part of the Louisiana Purchase, where America bought a fifth of their entire country from French ownership for 27¹/₄ million dollars, roughly three cents an acre. It is worth pointing out that the reason the French were willing to sell the land is because Napoleon was fighting Britain and desperately needed money.

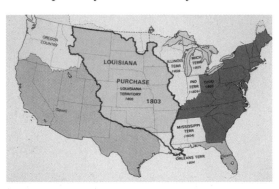

 Philogonius, Dominic of Silos.

21 DECEMBER

Midwinter's Day. (Mid*summer* in Australia.) The winter solstice, or shortest day. Also known as the festival of the Holly King, just as the summer solstice is traditionally the festival of the Oak King.

WINTER SOLSTICE
SHORTEST DAY

 Thomas, Peter Canisius.

22 DECEMBER

In 1715, James Stuart, the Catholic 'Old Pretender', lands at Peterhead to begin the first Jacobite rebellion against George I. The attempt to restore the Stuart line to the thrones of England and Scotland fails.

Ischyrian, Frances Cabrini.

23 DECEMBER

Sometimes known as 'Little Christmas', when festivities begin. On this day in 1688, James II, a Catholic, is deposed when a male heir is born who might create a new line of English Catholicism. James flees to France and William of Orange from Holland is asked to take the throne. William is married to James II's daughter, Mary. At first, they rule jointly as William III and Mary II, until Mary dies of smallpox in 1694. They had no heirs, so the throne passed to Anne, another daughter of James II.

John of Kanti, Thorlac.

24 DECEMBER

In 1166, King John, son of Henry II, is born at Beaumont Palace in Oxford. He will become the king of England and Ireland, but is most famous for being forced to seal the Magna Carta.

On this day in 1914, the first German air raid on British mainland takes place. An FF29 seaplane scored one hit on a church in Dover. There were no casualties, but some windows were broken and the gas-stove in a greenhouse was extinguished.

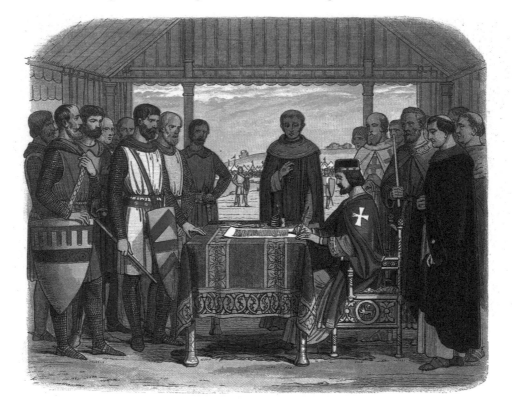

 Charbel Makhlouf.

25 DECEMBER

The Nativity of Christ and traditionally the final English Quarter Day. Sometimes written as 'Xmas' from the ancient practice of using a cross as a symbol for the word 'Christ'. Today, two billion people (one third of the world's population) celebrate the birth of Christ on this day.

'Here is a man who was born in an obscure village, the child of a peasant woman. He grew up in another obscure village. He worked in a carpenter's shop until he was thirty, and then for three years he was an itinerant preacher. He never wrote a book. He never held an office. He never owned a home… Yet I am far within the mark when I say that all the armies that have ever marched and all the navies that were ever built, and all the parliaments that ever sat, and all the kings that ever reigned, put together have not affected the life of man upon this earth as powerfully as has that one solitary life.' (From *The Gospels – a First Commentary* by F.G Herod, published by Methuen)

On this day in 1066, William the Conqueror is crowned in Westminster Abbey. His claim to the throne is partly through conquest, though he claims to have been offered the throne at different times by both Edward the Confessor and Harold Godwinson.

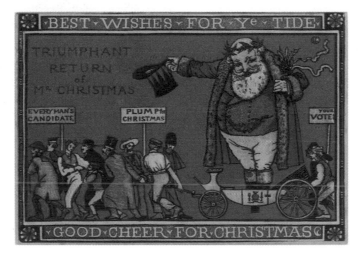

 Anastasia, Eugenia.

26 DECEMBER

Boxing Day celebrated as St Stephen's day in many countries. There are various theories about the origin of the name Boxing Day. One comes from the fact that servants were given their presents in boxes on this day – the servants' Christmas.

On this day in 1791, Charles Babbage is born in Teignmouth. He will go on to invent the calculating machine that was the fore-runner of computers.

Stephen, whose stoning was witnessed by St. Paul, which influenced his conversion to Christianity.

27 DECEMBER

In 1831, Charles Darwin sets sail in HMS *Beagle* on his journey to the Galapagos Islands. His discoveries there will inform and influence his theory of evolution.

Fabiola. Also John the Divine, brother to James and writer of the fourth gospel and the book of Revelation, written while he was in exile on the island of Patmos.

28 DECEMBER

In 1065, the consecration of Westminster Abbey in London takes place. The first king to be crowned there is Harold II, who will go on to lose the Battle of Hastings. The next king to be crowned there is William I (seen below), better known as William the Conqueror.

The Holy Innocents – the children of Bethlehem killed by King Herod.

29 DECEMBER

In 1170, the murder is committed of Thomas à Becket, the Archbishop of Canterbury. He is killed by four knights at an altar in Canterbury Cathedral, later to become a place of pilgrimage until Henry VIII had the remains burnt. King Henry II, having been denied revenues by Thomas, shouted, 'Who will rid me of this turbulent priest?' and the four knights set out, believing they were doing his bidding. After the murder, Henry II submits to being whipped in public as penance for his part in the murder.

Marcellus the Righteous. Also Thomas à Becket the Archbishop of Canterbury, who was killed on the order of Henry II in 1170 at Canterbury Cathedral.

30 DECEMBER

In 1916, the 'mad monk' Grigory Rasputin is killed, a surprisingly difficult thing to accomplish. He had become a guru to the Russian tsar and his family and was considered by some to be a malign influence on them. A group of nobles poison Rasputin's wine and food, but he thrives on it. When that fails, they shoot him and he collapses. To their astonishment, he comes round quickly, leaps up and half-strangles one of his assailants before trying to flee the palace grounds. He is shot three more times in the process, which doesn't stop him. The final attempt involves tying him up and throwing him into a freezing river. His body is later recovered and the official cause of death given as drowning.

Egwin.

31 DECEMBER

New Year's Eve. Around this day in 1695, a window tax is introduced in Britain. It seemed obvious that the more windows a house had, the wealthier the owners had to be. An unforeseen side-effect of this tax was that many windows on large houses were bricked up by their irate owners.

Also on this day, in 1960, the farthing, or quarter penny, ceases to be legal tender after six hundred years in use.

 Columba of Sens, Melania the Younger, Pope Silvester I.

Notes

Winter tree © Nicolette Caven 2007

Winter The Midnight Service (w/c on gouache on paper). Stanley Cook. Getty Images
Skating, published by L. Prang and Co. (litho) by Henry Sandham (1842–1912).
Library of Congress, Washington D.C. USA/Bridgeman Art Library

January Fol.57v January: Janus (vellum) by Master Ermengaut (d.1322). Biblioteca
Monasterio del Escorial, Madrid, Spain. Giraudon/Bridgeman Art Library
Mr Punch Goes First Footing. *Punch's Almanac for 1897* in Punch vol. 112–113,
1897. Mary Evans Picture Library
Branch illo © Joy Gosney 2007
Duck illo © Joy Gosney 2007

1 Jan Gregoire XIII (Ugo Boncompagni, 1502–1585), pope from 1572 to 1585, promulgating the new calendar (1582). Tablet of Biccherna (1582–1583). Siena (Italy), State archives. Photo by Roger Viollet Collection/Getty Images

2 Jan Baron Robert Clive. Getty Images

3 Jan December 1955: John Ronald Reuel Tolkien (1892–1973), British writer and professor at Merton College Oxford, reading in his study. Haywood Magee/Picture Post/Getty Images

4 Jan Donald Campbell's *Bluebird* hits the wake and lifts off from Coniston Water (Cumbria, UK), somersaulting and disintegrating upon landing. Michael Brennan/CORBIS

5 Jan Portrait of Henry VIII (1491–1547) by Hans Holbein the Younger (1497/8–1543). Belvoir Castle, Leicestershire. UK/Bridgeman Art Library

6 Jan The Adoration of the Magi (oil on panel) by Jan Gossaert (Mabuse) (c.1472–c.1533). Museo Lazaro Galdiano, Madrid, Spain. Giraudon/Bridgeman Art Library

7 Jan Frontispiece of *Dialogus De Systemate Mundi* by Galileo (1564–1642), published in Leyden, 1635 (engraving) (b/w photo) by Dutch School. Bibliotheque Nationaule, Paris, France. Archives Charmet/Bridgeman Art Library

8 Jan King Alfred (849–899). Mary Evans Picture Library

9 Jan Funeral Procession of the late Viscount Nelson, engraved by Merigot, pub. 18; by Augustus Charles Pugin (1762–1832) (after). Guildhall Library, City of London/Bridgeman Art Library

10 Jan Head of Caesar Augustus. Private Collection/Bridgeman Art Library

11 Jan 1925 studio portrait of Thomas Hardy. Underwood & Underwood/Time & Life Pictures/Getty Images

12 Jan	Michael Caine in the film, *Zulu*. Ronald Grant Archive
13 Jan	Retreat from Kabul. National Army Museum, London, UK. Bridgeman Art Library
14 Jan	Bell telephone used by Queen Victoria at Osborne House, Isle of Wight, 1877–78. Science Museum, London, UK/Bridgeman Art Library
15 Jan	Lt Bligh and officers cast adrift from the *Bounty*. Aquatint by Robert Dodd. The Art Archive
16 Jan	Sir John Moore (1761–1809) at Corunna, from *British Battles on Land and Sea* edited by Sir Evelyn Wood. Private Collection/Bridgeman Art Library
17 Jan	United Kingdom Foreign Minister Ernest Bevin during the inaugural meeting of the United Nations Security Council. Erich Auerbach/Getty Images
18 Jan	*Boy's Own Paper* Saturday March 12 1892, *The Orchid Seekers: A Story of Adventure and Peril*. Vintage Magazine Archive
19 Jan	Canute shows that he cannot order back the waves. Date: c.1017. Mary Evans Picture Library
20 Jan	20 Oct 1936, King Edward and Wallis Simpson disembark from his chartered yacht at Rab, Yugoslavia. Bettmann/Corbis
21 Jan	George Orwell. Rex Features
22 Jan	Map of Rorke's Drift © John MacKenzie
23 Jan	A portrait of Salvador Dali (1904–89) taken January 1972 in Paris. STF/AFP/Getty Images
24 Jan	Funeral of Sir Winston Churchill, as the cortege arrives at St Paul's Cathedral. Fox Photos/Hulton/Getty Images
25 Jan	Robert Burns (1759–96), 1787 by Alexander Nasmyth (1758–1840). Scottish National Portrait Gallery, Edinburgh, Scotland/Bridgeman Art Library
26 Jan	Sydney Cove, 1794 by Thomas Watling (1762–1814). Bridgeman Art Library
27 Jan	A pile of human bones and skulls at the Nazi concentration camp of Majdanek following its liberation in 1944. AFP/Getty Images
28 Jan	Henry VII from The Great Window of St Margaret's Church, Westminster. National Portrait Gallery
29 Jan	Victoria Cross, the New Order of Valour for the Army, c.1856 (engraving) by English School. Private Collection/The Stapleton Collection/Bridgeman Art Library
30 Jan	Execution of King Charles I. Mary Evans Picture Library
31 Jan	The Gunpowder Plot Conspirators, 1606 (engraving) (later colouration) by German School. Private Collection/Bridgeman Art Library
February	St. Valentine (painted glass) by Hungarian School (19th century). Private Collection/Archives Charmet/Bridgeman Art Library
	Grand Parade, 2004 (acrylic on canvas & wood) by P.J. Crook (b.1945). Private Collection/Bridgeman Art Library
	Pancake illo © Joy Gosney
1 Feb	A close-up of a set of the new English coins minted for the reign of King George VI, including a crown, a half crown, a two shilling piece, a shilling, a sixpence, a three pence or thrupenny bit, a penny, a half penny or ha'penny and a farthing. Central Press/Getty Images
2 Feb	November–December 1942, USSR. Long march of POWs from the Battle of Stalingrad. Dmitri Baltermants/The Dmitri Baltermants Collection/Corbis

3 Feb	*Luna 9*, January 9, 1966. RIA /Novosti
4 Feb	United States Stamp (George Washington). Bettmann/Corbis
5 Feb	The Royal Extinguisher or The King of Brobdingnag and the Lilliputians, 1821 by G. Cruikshank. Guildhall Library, City of London/Bridgeman Art Library
6 Feb	St George's Chapel, Windsor. Rex Features
7 Feb	Charles Dickens (1812–1870). Mansell/Time Life Pictures/Getty Images
8 Feb	Mary Tudor. Mary Evans Picture Library
9 Feb	Walter Swinburn of Great Britain on Shergar during the King George VI and Queen Elizabeth Diamond Stakes at Ascot. Allsport/Getty Images
10 Feb	Treaty of Paris, signed by France, Great Britain & Spain. Archives du Ministere des Affaires Etrangeres, Paris, France. Archives Charmet/Bridgeman Art Library
11 Feb	Poster for *The 39 Steps*, 1935, starring Madeleine Carroll and Robert Donat. Ronald Grant Archive
12 Feb	Portrait of Charles Robert Darwin (1809–82), English naturalist (oil on panel) by English School. South African National Gallery, Cape Town, South Africa/Bridgeman Art Library
13 Feb	Massacre of Glencoe (oil on canvas) by James Hamilton (1853–94). Art Gallery and Museum, Kelvingrove, Glasgow, Scotland/Glasgow City Council/Bridgeman Art Library
14 Feb	Captain Cook is killed in Hawaii. Mary Evans Picture Library
15 Feb	Decimal currency. Rex Features
16 Feb	Three women and their coloured nylon stockings. Original Publication: Picture Post. Raymond Kleboe/Getty Images
17 Feb	Geronimo (c.1829–1909). Hulton Archive/Getty Images
18 Feb	Clyde Tombaugh (1906–1997) with the blink comparator he used to discover Pluto. Science Photo Library
19 Feb	The Copernican System, *Planisphaerium Copernicanum*, c.1543, devised by Nicolaus Copernicus (1473–1543) from *The Celestial Atlas, or the Harmony of the Universe* (*Atlas coelestis seu harmonia macrocosmica*) Amsterdam, c.1660, Cellarius, Andreas. British Library, London/Bridgeman Art Library
20 Feb	Lord Louis Mountbatten (1900–1979). Fox Photos/Getty Images
21 Feb	World War II identity cards. Mary Evans Picture Library
22 Feb	The Hall of Mysteries, Pompeii, 79 AD (wall painting), Roman. Museo e Gallerie Nazionali di Capodimonte, Naples, Italy/Bridgeman Art Library
23 Feb	James Augustus Grant (left) with Speke, in Africa in 1863. Mary Evans Picture Library
24 Feb	Charles, Prince of Wales, with his fiancée Lady Diana Spencer (1961–1997) after announcing their engagement. Hulton Archive/Getty Images
25 Feb	St Paul's Cathedral. Mary Evans Picture Library
26 Feb	Dr Robert Runcie, Archbishop of Canterbury ordains the first woman priests in Canterbury Cathedral. Keystone/Hulton Archive/Getty Images
27 Feb	Napoleon I (1769–1821) as Emperor after 1804. Mary Evans Picture Library
28 Feb	The Relief of Ladysmith (oil on canvas) by John Henry Frederick Bacon (1868–1914). Courtesy of the Council, National Army Museum, London/Bridgeman Art Library
29 Feb	'A solemn warning to single men.' Ladies take advantage of the custom of proposing to men on 29 February. Mary Evans Picture Library

March	Copper plate etching showing Roman god Mars, god of war and father of Romulus and Remus, from *The War Habits of the Romans* (*Der Kriegswesen der Romer*), 1824. Mansell/Time Life Pictures/Getty Images
	Sword and helmet illo © Joy Gosney 2007
1 Mar	St David illo © Nicolette Caven 2007
2 Mar	Concorde taking off, 1985. Peter Brooker/Rex Features
3 Mar	The meeting between Henry VIII and Francois I, on the Field of the Cloth of Gold, 7 June 1520. Mary Evans Picture Library
4 Mar	The Enigma code machine, developed by H.A. Koch in 1919 and used by German intelligence up to World War II. Hulton Archive/Getty Images
5 Mar	Coat of arms of the Norman Kings. Wiedenfeld & Nicolson
6 Mar	Sistine Chapel Ceiling (1508–12): The Creation of Adam, 1511–12 (fresco) (post restoration), Buonarroti, Michelangelo (1475–1564). Vatican Museums and Galleries, Vatican City, Italy/Bridgeman Art Library
7 Mar	Admiral Horatio Nelson's flagship HMS *Victory* being towed into Gibraltar and later moored at Portsmouth. Also shown are the semaphore flags with which Nelson signalled his fleet before the battle of Trafalgar: 'England Expects That Every Man Will Do His Duty'. Hulton Archive/Getty Images
8 Mar	Reverse of medal commemorating the Battle of Beachy Head, with portrait of King William III. British Museum, London, UK/Bridgeman Art Library
9 Mar	The USS *Monitor* fighting the CSS *Merrimack* at the Battle of Hampton Roads during the American Civil War, by American School. Private Collection. Peter Newark Military Pictures/Bridgeman Art library
10 Mar	Alexander Graham Bell (1847–1922, centre) performing the first long-distance telephone call in 1876. The conversation took place between Boston, Massachusetts, USA, and the town of Salem, some 13 miles away. Illustration taken from *La Telegraphie Historique* (1888) by Alexis Belloc. Science Photo Library
11 Mar	One pound note and one pound coin. Nils Jorgensen/Rex Features
12 Mar	Yehudi Menuhin on the South Bank Show, Mar 1990. Rex Features
13 Mar	Earl Grey Tea Pack from 1931. Twining's Catalogue. R. Twining and Co. Ltd
14 Mar	Albert Einstein (1879–1955). Photographed by a fellow student at the Zurich Polytechnic Institute, Switzerland, between 1896–1900. Science Photo Library
15 Mar	Marlon Brando in the film of *Julius Caesar*, 1953. Ronald Grant Archive
16 Mar	The members of Captain Scott's ill-fated expedition to the South Pole: (l to r) Laurence Oates, H.R. Bowers, Robert Scott, Edward Wilson and Edgar Evans. They reached the Pole a month after Roald Amundsen's Norwegian party, but all died on the return journey. Bettmann/Corbis
17 Mar	St Patrick illo © Nicolette Caven 2007
18 Mar	10 Downing Street. Mary Evans Picture Library
19 Mar	Sir Richard Francis Burton. Ernest Edwards/Getty Images
20 Mar	Million pound note illo © Joy Gosney 2007
21 Mar	Equinox illo © Joy Gosney 2007
22 Mar	King Charles II by John Michael Wright. National Portrait Gallery
23 Mar	Russia's Mir Space Station backdropped against a cloud-covered Earth. NASA/Science Photo Library
24 Mar	Queen Elizabeth I, c.1585–90 (panel) by John the Younger Bettes (c.1530–1615/6). Private Collection/Bridgeman Art Library

25 Mar	1st Battalion 6th Gurkha Rifles led by Major C.J.L. Allanson attacking the Turks on the crest of Sari Bair ridge, Gallipoli, 9 August 1916, 1981 (oil on canvas), Terence Cuneo (1907–96). Gurkha Museum, Winchester, England/Bridgeman Art Library
26 Mar	Cecil Rhodes (1853–1902) in South Africa, making peace with the Matabele, 1896. Mary Evans Picture Library
27 Mar	King Charles I (1600–49) (oil on canvas) by Sir Anthony van Dyck (1599–1641). Burghley House Collection, Lincolnshire, UK/Bridgeman Art Library
28 Mar	Santa Sophia mosque and fishing boats on the shore of the Bosphorus, Istanbul. Private Collection. The Stapleton Collection/Bridgeman Art Library
29 Mar	In the Temple gardens, London, the Duke of York picks a white rose, the Duke of Lancaster prefers the red. And so a legend is born and a nasty war gets a pretty name. Date: c.1455. Mary Evans Picture Library
30 Mar	A Short Stirling Bomber being serviced. Fox Photos/Getty Images
31 Mar	Promotional card for 'Beensdorp' chocolate with an illustration of Sir Isaac Newton (1642–1727) making his discovery of the Universal Law of Gravitation. Early 20th century (colour litho) by French School. Private Collection/Archives Charmet/Bridgeman Art Library
Spring tree	© Nicolette Caven 2007
Spring	Easy Lawn Mower advert. Museum of Rural Life, University of Reading
	Boys playing marbles illo © Joy Gosney 2007
April	The Birth of Venus, c.1865–69 (oil on canvas) by Alexandre Cabanel (1823–89) and Adolphe Jourdan (1825–89). Dahesh Museum of Art, New York, USA/Bridgeman Art Library
	A couple and their son rejoice as the first seed sprouts in their allotment. Date: early 20th century. Source: Unattributed design on a postcard in the Steve Rumney Collection. Mary Evans Picture Library
	Eggs and beans illos © Joy Gosney 2007
	Peas and horses illos © Joy Gosney 2007
1 Apr	Print of the Royal Air Force Badge. Stapleton Collection/Corbis
2 Apr	Falklands flag
3 Apr	Jesse James. SNAP/Rex Features
4 Apr	Francis Drake and the Golden Hind. Ron Embleton (1930–88). Look and Learn Magazine Ltd/Bridgeman Art Library
5 Apr	Operating table. Surgical operating table used in Glasgow, Scotland by Baron Joseph Lister (1827–1912). Science Photo Library
6 Apr	A worker prepares a stage with a display of the Olympic rings at the Raffles City Convention Centre in Singapore July 5, 2005. Bazuki Muhammad/Reuters/Corbis
7 Apr	Dick Turpin (1706–39) from *Peeps into the Past*, published c.1900 (colour litho) by Trelleek. Private Collection/The Stapleton Collection/Bridgeman Art Library
8 Apr	Great Western Steamer. Cigarette Card in Will's Celebrated Ships series (1911). Mary Evans Picture Library
9 Apr	Family tree © Graeme Andrew
10 Apr	The sinking of *Titanic* by Henry Reuterdahl based on material supplied by survivors of the shipwreck. Mansell/Time Life Pictures/Getty Images

11 Apr	Singapore flag. Stocbyte/PunchStock
12 Apr	Yuri Gagarin. Bettmann/Corbis
13 Apr	Sir Arthur T. Harris (1892–1984). Hulton-Deutsch Collection/Corbis
14 Apr	*Apollo 13* spacecraft lifting off from Launch Pad A at Cape Kennedy Space Centre. Time Life Pictures/NASA/Time Life Pictures/Getty Images
15 Apr	*Boston Daily Globe*. Rex Features
16 Apr	The final charge of the Royal troops, commanded by the Duke of Cumberland, leading to total victory over the forces of the Young Pretender. Mary Evans Picture Library
17 Apr	Cuban leader Fidel Castro (b.1926/27) watching a baseball game, one of his favourite sports. Popperfoto
18 Apr	Albert Einstein demonstrates mathematical formulas on a blackboard in front of Californian scientists. Bettmann/Corbis
19 Apr	Postcard of Lord Byron by an unnamed artist probably based on an engraving by G. Sanders. Mary Evans Picture Library
20 Apr	English warships under Admiral Blake in action against the French at Santa Cruz. Mary Evans Picture Library
21 Apr	She Wolf, c.500 BC with figures of Romulus and Remus by Antonio Pollaiuolo (1433–98) c.1484–96 (bronze) by Etruscan (6th century BC). Museo Capitolino, Rome, Italy/Bridgeman Art Library
22 Apr	Train in the Snow or The Locomotive, 1875 (oil on canvas) by Claude Monet (1840–1926). Musee Marmottan, Paris, France/Giraudon/Bridgeman Art Library
23 Apr	St George illo © Nicolette Caven 2007
24 Apr	British Prime Minister Sir Winston Leonard Spencer Churchill (1874–1965). Hulton Archive/Getty Images
25 Apr	Portrait of Oliver Cromwell (1599–1658) 1649 (oil on canvas) by Robert Walker (1607–60). Leeds Museums and Galleries (City Art Gallery)/Bridgeman Art Library
26 Apr	Extract showing John Smith from Map of the Coast of New England, Observed and Described by Captain John Smith 1614, from *Generall Historie*, 1624 (engraving) (b&w photo), Passe, Simon de (1595–1647). Library of Congress, Washington D.C., USA/Bridgeman Art Library
27 Apr	Video grab of Betty Boothroyd, marking her retirement as Speaker of the House of Commons with a valedictory speech to MPs. PA Archive/PA Photos
28 Apr	Queen Victoria as Empress of India, 1887. Mary Evans Picture Library
29 Apr	Dachau, Bavaria, Germany. Concentration camp prisoners smile and wave a US flag as US troops liberate the Nazi concentration camp in Dachau, Germany, 30 April 1945. Corbis
30 Apr	A helicopter on top of a building in Saigon as evacuees scramble up a ladder to the roof to flee from the city. Popperfoto
May	Pomona, 1884–85 (wool and silk tapestry made by Morris & Co.) by Edward Burne-Jones (1833–98) & William Morris (1834–96). Whitworth Art Gallery. The University of Manchester, UK/Bridgeman Art Library
	Raising the pole. Date: 1882. Source: N Casella, cover for *The Maypole*. Mary Evans Picture Library
	Motorbike illo © Joy Gosney
1 May	Flag of England. Altrendo images/Getty Images

2 May	DCO1. Dyson Ltd
3 May	Emperor Hirohito in morning clothes standing next to visiting General Douglas MacArthur. US Army Signal Corps/US Army Signal Corps/Time & Life Pictures/Getty Images
4 May	The Spirit of Ecstasy, the prestigious marque of the Rolls Royce motor car. Paul Vicente/AFP/Getty Images
5 May	Commandos about to enter the Iranian embassy. STF/AFP/Getty Images
6 May	The Penny Black. Hulton Archive/Getty Images
7 May	Sketch done at time of the *Lusitania* disaster, May 1915. Time Life Pictures/Mansell/Time Life Pictures/Getty Images
8 May	From a balcony in Whitehall, Churchill addresses a huge crowd. Bettmann/Corbis
9 May	Regalia as worn in the coronation: Ampulla, St Edward's Crown, Queen Mary II's Sceptre with Dove, Sovereign's Orb, Queen Mary II's Sceptre with Dove, Jewelled Sword of Offering, Armills, Spurs, Sovereign's Ring, Sovereign's Sceptre with Cross. Crown © The Royal Collection © Her Majesty Queen Elizabeth II
10 May	Winston Churchill. Central Press/Getty Images
11 May	English Prime Minister Spencer Perceval being assassinated in the lobby of the House of Commons, London. Hulton Archive/Getty Images
12 May	Map by Ken Lewis
13 May	Pope John Paul II celebrates Mass at Downsview Park in Toronto, Canada. Rex Features
14 May	Map by Andrew Ashton © HarperCollins*Publishers*
15 May	Nuclear Explosion South Pacific. Rex Features
16 May	Deputy Prime Minister John Prescott in Rhyl. David Kendall/PA Photos
17 May	*The Dambusters* film, 1955. Ronald Grant Archive
18 May	The launching of English fireships on the Spanish fleet off Calais with Queen Elizabeth I (1533–1603) on horseback on shore, by Flemish School. Private Collection/Bridgeman Art Library
19 May	Anne Boleyn (1507–36) in the Tower, detail, 1835 (oil on canvas) by Edouard Cibot (Francois Berthelemy Michel) (1799–1877). Musee Rolin, Autun, France/Bridgeman Art Library
20 May	John Stuart Mill. The photograph was probably taken shortly after the death of his wife. Stereoscopic Company/Getty Images
21 May	British naval commander William Hobson (1793–1842), c.1840. Hulton Archive/Getty Images
22 May	Family tree © Graeme Andrew
23 May	Gallows for execution by beheading. Mansell/Time & Life Pictures/Getty Images
24 May	Dodo. Stock Montage/Getty Images
25 May	The Venerable Bede. Mary Evans Picture Library
26 May	The Bottomless Pitt – satirical cartoon published in 1792 of William Pitt the Younger by James Gillray. British Library, London, UK/Bridgeman Art Library
27 May	The Last of the *Bismarck*: Shelled, Bombed, and on Fire, the Nazi Mammoth is Torpedoed by HMS *Dorsetshire*, from *The Illustrated London News*, 7 June 1941 (litho), Charles Eddowes Turner (1883–1965). Private Collection/Bridgeman Art Library

28 May	A line of British soldiers advancing during the Falklands War. Hulton Archive/Getty Images
29 May	Tenzing Norgay on the Summit of Mount Everest. Tenzing waves his ice-axe on which are hung the flags of Britain, Nepal, the United Nations and India. Edmund Hilary/Royal Geographical Society
30 May	Portrait of Joan of Arc (1412–1431) entitled *La Prophetie De Merlin* (The Prophesy of Merlin). Mansell/Time Life Pictures/Getty Images
31 May	Big Ben. Rex Features
June	Juno. Illustration by Walter Crane, in *Baby's Own Aesop*, 1887. Mary Evans Picture Library
	Stonehenge, or a Circular Temple of the Druids, plate 19 from *The History of the Nations* (aquatint) by Italian School (19th century). Private Collection/The Stapleton Collection/Bridgeman Art Library
	Tennis racket and cricket bat illos © Joy Gosney 2007
1 Jun	Sir Frank Whittle. Rex Features
2 Jun	Queen Elizabeth II, Archbishop of Canterbury Dr Geoffrey Fisher and dignitaries at the Coronation, Westminster Abbey. Reg Speller/Hulton Archive/Getty Images
3 Jun	Portrait of George V (1865–1936), 1926 (oil on canvas), Richard Jack, (1866–1952). Private Collection/The Fine Art Society, London, UK/Bridgeman Art Library
4 Jun	Family tree © Graeme Andrew
5 Jun	Christine Keeler after leaving court during the Stephen Ward case. Fred Mott/Getty Images
7 Jun	Illustration of the Battle of Midway, 1942. Hulton Archive/Getty Images
8 June	Edward VI with the chain of the Order of the Garter, after the portrait in the Collection of H.M. Queen Elizabeth II, c.1600 4 by William Scrots. Private Collection/Richard Philp, London/Bridgeman Art Library
9 Jun	Twenty pence coin. Rex Features
10 Jun	Gold Badge. Duke of Edinburgh Award Scheme
11 Jun	Henry VIII (1491–1547) and Catherine of Aragon (1485–1536) before the Papal Legates at Blackfriars in 1529, 1910 (oil on canvas), Frank Cadogan Cowper (1877–1958). Palace of Westminster, London, UK/Bridgeman Art Library
12 Jun	Swiss Amy knife. Victorinox
13 Jun	Alexander the Great wearing a ram's horns as a sign of his divinity. Date: 356–323 BC. Mary Evans Picture Library
14 Jun	Three Men in a Boat (gouache on paper), Paul Rainer (20th century). Private Collection/Look and Learn/Bridgeman Art Library
15 Jun	Death of Wat Tyler. British Library, London, UK/Bridgeman Art Library
16 Jun	Valentina Tereshkova practises feeding in simulated flight conditions. Keystone/Getty Images
17 Jun	Caernarvon Castle, 1792 (oil on canvas) by Julius Caesar Ibbetson (1759–1817). National Museum and Gallery of Wales, Cardiff/Bridgeman Art Library
18 Jun	The Battle of Waterloo (oil on canvas) by Robert Alexander Hillingford (1825–1904). Private Collection. Bridgeman Art Library
19 Jun	Copy of the Magna Carta (whole sheet). Lincoln Cathedral, Lincolnshire, UK/Bridgeman Art Library

20 Jun	South East View of Kensington Palace, 1826 (w/c on paper), John Buckler (1770–1851). Private Collection/Bridgeman Art Library
21 Jun	Solstice illo © Joy Gosney 2007
22 Jun	Joe Louis (Joseph Louis Barrow) (1914–1981). Bettmann/Corbis
23 Jun	The Battle of Plassey of 1757 (gouache on paper), Peter Jackson (1922–2003). Private Collection © Look and Learn/Bridgeman Art Library
24 Jun	Battle of Ecluse. Bibliotheque Nationale, Paris, France/DACS/Bridgeman Art Library
25 Jun	Custer's last stand at the Battle of Little Bighorn (colour litho) by American School (19th century). Private Collection/Peter Newark American Pictures/ Bridgeman Art Library
26 Jun	Windsor Castle. Rex Features
27 Jun	Portrait of Prince Charles Edward Louis Philip Casimir Stewart (1720–88), the Young Pretender or 'Bonnie Prince Charlie'. Litho by the English School (19th century). Private Collection/Bridgeman Art Library
28 Jun	*New York Times*. John Frost Newspaper Collection
29 Jun	St Peter illo © Nicolette Caven 2007
30 Jun	Sixpence. Central Press/Getty Images

Summer tree © Nicolette Caven 2007	
Summer	Boat illo © Joy Gosney 2007
	Family travel to the seaside by motor car. Date: c.1929. Savile Lumley in *My Travel Book by Land Sea & Air*. Mary Evans Picture Library

July	'I don't care twopence what happens. That's how I feel at Clacton-on-Sea.' Date: 20th century. Steve Rumney Collection. Unattributed postcard. Mary Evans Picture Library
	Oxford: punting near Magdalen College bridge. Date: c.1905. Unattributed photograph on a postcard. Mary Evans Picture Library
1 Jul	Canadian Flag. Getty Images
2 Jul	Battle of Marston Moor by John Barker (19th century). Cheltenham Art Gallery & Museums, Gloucestershire, UK/Bridgeman Art Library
3 Jul	British bombers attack French warships in the harbour of Oran, Algeria, to prevent them being used by the Germans. Date: 1940. Mary Evans Picture Library
4 Jul	Declaration of Independence document, 1776. Mary Evans Picture Library
5 Jul	Dolly the Sheep. Getty Images
6 Jul	Sir Thomas More and his daughter Margaret Roper at his prison window during his imprisonment for high treason. They are watching monks going to their execution. Original Artwork: Engraved by R Anderson. Hulton Archive/Getty Images
7 Jul	Queen Elizabeth I (1530–1603) knights Francis Drake (1540–96), illustration *from Heroes of History* (colour litho) by Howard Davie. Private Collection/ Bridgeman Art Library
8 Jul	French fighter Charlemont introduces a little Gallic flair to the boxing ring. Driscoll maintains a stiff upper lip. Unattributed illustration in *Le Petit Journal* 12 November 1899. Mary Evans Picture Library
9 Jul	Maureen O'Sullivan and Johnny Weissmuller in *Tarzan's Secret Treasure*. Aquarius Collection

10 Jul	Portrait of Lady Jane Grey (1537–54) 'Nine-Days Queen' from *Memoirs of the Court of Queen Elizabeth*, published in 1825 (w/c and gouache on paper), Sarah Countess of Essex (d.1838). Private Collection, The Stapleton Collection/Bridgeman Art Library
11 Jul	Robert the Bruce. Mary Evans Picture Library
12 Jul	HMS *Victory* sailing for the French line flanked by the *Euryalus* and HMS *Temeraire* at the Battle of Trafalgar by Thomas Whitcombe (c.1752–1824). Private Collection/The Stapleton Collection/Bridgeman Art Library
13 Jul	Royalist cavalry at the Battle of Marston Moor in 1644, 1819 (oil on canvas), Abraham Cooper (1787–1868). Harris Museum and Art Gallery, Preston, Lancashire, UK/Bridgeman Art Library
14 Jul	Dynamite. Getty Images Alfred Nobel (1833–96) (engraving) (b/w photo) by French School (19th century). Bibliotheque de la Faculte de Medecine, Paris, France/Archives. Charmet/Bridgeman Art Library
15 Jul	St Swithin's Memorial. Winchester Cathedral
16 Jul	Apollo 11 crew: Neil Armstrong, Commander, Michael Collins, Module Pilot, Buzz Aldrin, Lunar Module Pilot. NASA
17 Jul	Weighing scales. Science Photo Library
18 Jul	John Glenn. Washington 1998. Rex Features
19 Jul	The Rosetta Stone, from Fort St. Julien, El-Rashid (Rosetta) 196 BC by Ptolemaic Period Egyptian (332–30 BC). British Museum, London, UK/Bridgeman Art Library
20 Jul	Neil Armstrong walking on the surface of the moon during the *Apollo 11* mission. Time Life Pictures/NASA/Time Life Pictures/Getty Images
21 Jul	Henry IV Part I Title page. Private Collection
22 Jul	Battle of Salamanca, published 1821 (aquatint) by William Heath (1795–1840). Courtesy of the Council, National Army Museum, London, UK/Bridgeman Art Library
23 Jul	Sir William Ramsay presenting a lecture. Illustration taken from *Vanity Fair* in the 1890s. Science Photo Library
24 Jul	Mary Queen of Scots (1542–87), dated 1578, painted c.1610/15, Anonymous. Scottish National Portrait Gallery, Edinburgh, Scotland/Bridgeman Art Library
25 Jul	St Christopher illo © Nicolette Caven 2007
26 Jul	Aldous Huxley typing at desk. Eric Schaal/Time Life Pictures/Getty Images
27 Jul	Sir Walter Raleigh enjoys his pipe. Date: c.1600. © Mary Evans Picture Library
28 Jul	James Watson (b.1928), left, and Francis Crick (b.1916), with their model of part of a DNA molecule in 1953. Barrington Brown/Science Photo Library
29 Jul	*The Fellowship of the Rings* cover, dust jacket design by J.R.R. Tolkien. © HarperCollins*Publishers*
30 Jul	England World Cup Winners 1966 – Bobby Moore © Sporting Pictures UK, Ltd. Action Images/Sporting Pictures
31 Jul	A detective leads Doctor Hawley Harvey Crippen (1862–1910) from the SS *Megantic*, August 1910. He had attempted to flee the country after murdering his wife, but was apprehended with the use of radio communication, tried and executed. Photo by Hulton Archive/Getty Images.

August	Head of Emperor Augustus (63 BC–14 AD) crowned with an oak wreath (stone) (detail) by Roman. Louvre, Paris, France
	Seashore Shenanigans, 1990. Jane Wooster Scott/Superstock
1 Aug	Robert Stephenson Smyth, 1st Baron Baden-Powell. Rischgitz/Getty Images
2 Aug	Cards © Andrew Ashton 2007
3 Aug	Hannibal famously used elephants in battle. Elephant illo © Joy Gosney 2007
5 Aug	American actress Marilyn Monroe (1926–1962) in a scene from *The Seven Year Itch* directed by Billy Wilder. MPI/Getty Images
6 Aug	US marines watch the mushroom cloud from an atomic explosion in Nevada during a US nuclear weapons test. Keystone/Getty Images
7 Aug	Family tree © Graeme Andrew
8 Aug	Paul Dirac. The blackboard displays a quantum mechanical model of the hydrogen molecule.. American Institute of Physics/Science Photo Library
9 Aug	Spartan Army (gouache on paper), Andrew Howat (20th Century). Private Collection/Look and Learn/Bridgeman Art Library
10 Aug	The Royal Observatory from Greenwich Park. Date: c.1850. Unattributed engraving in *The Leisure Hour*. Mary Evans Picture Library
11 Aug	*Five on a Secret Trail*
12 Aug	Grouse moor at Balmoral. Mary Evans Picture Library
13 Aug	Portrait of King Henry V (1387–1422) (oil on canvas) by Benjamin Burnell (1769–1828). Private Collection/Philip Mould Ltd, London/Bridgeman Art Library
14 Aug	A sailor and nurse embrace in New York's Times Square. Victor Jorgensen/AP Photos
15 Aug	Colonel Thomas Edward Lawrence (1888–1935), better known as Lawrence of Arabia. Hulton Archive/Getty Images
16 Aug	Elvis Presley in *Jailhouse Rock*. Rex Features
17 Aug	A petrol-powered Panhard Levassor Phaeton with starting handle, 1896 (coloured b/w photo), French School. Bibliotheque des Arts Decoratifs, Paris, France, Archives Charmet/Bridgeman Art Library
18 Aug	Genghis Khan. Mary Evans Picture Library
19 Aug	An interior view of Boulton and Watt's steam engine works at Soho, Birmingham. Mary Evans Picture Library
20 Aug	Stainless steel spoon. Superstock
21 Aug	St. Sebastian, 31 August 1813, from *The Victories of the Duke of Wellington*, engraved by T. Fielding, pub. 1819, coloured by Richard Westall (1765–1836). Private Collection/The Stapleton Collection/Bridgeman Art Library
22 Aug	Henry Maudslay (1771–1831). Science Photo Library
23 Aug	Statue of William Wallace, National Wallace Monument, Stirling, Scotland. Rex Features
24 Aug	Remains of one of Pompeii's human victims. Mary Evans Picture Library
25 Aug	JCB *Dieselmax* breaks SCTA diesel car speed record. Tim Scott/Fluid Images/Rex Features
26 Aug	Coat of arms of Edward III. Wiedenfeld & Nicolson
27 Aug	Clouds pouring from Krakatoa. Royal Society Report on Krakatoa Eruption, pub. 1888. Lithograph Parker & Coward. Hulton Archive/Getty Images
28 Aug	Cetewayo kaMpande (c.1832–1884). Henry Guttmann/Getty Images

29 Aug	Portrait of Michael Faraday. Science Photo Library
30 Aug	*Frankenstein* starring Boris Karloff, 1931. Everett Collection/Rex Features
31 Aug	Flowers outside Kensington Palace after the death of Princess Diana. Tony Kyriacou/Rex Features
September	Oysters. Mary Evans Picture Library
	Dick Whittington and his cat. From an English chapbook, 17th century. Bettmann/Corbis
	Horse and branch illos © Joy Gosney 2007
1 Sep	*The Evening News.* John Frost Newspaper Collection
2 Sep	The Great Fire of London, 1666 by Dutch School. Museum of London, UK/ Bridgeman Art Library
3 Sep	British Prime Minister Neville Chamberlain (1869–1940) in a BBC studio announcing the declaration of war. Fox Photos/Getty Images
4 Sep	Map © Leslie Robinson
5 Sep	A French map of Washington's victory over Cornwallis at the Battle of Yorktown in 1781. Corbis
6 Sep	The Great Fire, 1666 (coloured engraving), Doornik, Marcus Willemsz (17th century). Guildhall Library, City of London/Bridgeman Art Library
7 Sep	Queen Mary (1516–58) and Princess Elizabeth (1533–1603) entering London, 1553, 1910, John Byam Liston Shaw (1872–1919). Houses of Parliament, Westminster, London, UK/Bridgeman Art Library
8 Sep	Crusaders under Richard 1192. Unattributed illustration in *British History in Periods Book 4*, p99. Mary Evans Picture Library
9 Sep	*Mutiny on the Bounty* 1962. Starring Marlon Brando as Christian Fletcher and Trevor Howard as William Bligh. Ronald Grant Archive
10 Sep	A motor hansom cab on a standard 1905 Vauxhall chassis with the controls changed over so the driver can operate them from the rear and aloft. Hulton Archive/Getty Images
11 Sep	World Trade Centre disaster. Erik C Pendzich/Rex Features
12 Sep	President Bush looks down as he makes a statement regarding the terrorist acts upon the World Trade Centre. Chris O'Meara/AP
13 Sep	The Death of General Wolfe (1727–59), c.1771 (oil on panel) by Benjamin West (1738–1820). Private Collection/Phillips/Bridgeman Art Library
14 Sep	A postal stamp dedicated to the *Luna 2* launch, September 14, 1959. RIA Novosti
15 Sep	Four naval Seafire Spitfires. Central Press/Getty Images
16 Sep	Earth. Satellite image of the Earth, centred on North Africa. Science Photo Library
17 Sep	The drafting of the Declaration of Independence. From l–r: Benjamin Franklin, Thomas Jefferson, John Adams, Robert Livingston and Roger Sherman. Stock Montage/Getty Images
18 Sep	Title page of Volume I of *The English Dictionary* by Dr Samuel Johnson (1709–84), pub. 1755. Private Collection/Bridgeman Art Library
19 Sep	Edward the Black Prince (1330–76): effigy in Canterbury Cathedral (gilt bronze). Cathedral, Kent, UK/Bridgeman Art Library
20 Sep	The 23rd Royal Welsh Fusiliers at the Battle of Alma (w/c) by English School. Private Collection/Bridgeman Art Library

21 Sep	Portrait of King Edward II (1284–1327) by J. Smith (engraving) (b/w photo) by English School (19th century). Private Collection/Bridgeman Art Library
22 Sep	Faraday's electrolysis experiment. The test tube (lower right) contains two platinum electrodes dipped in molten tin chloride heated by a spirit lamp. The electrodes are connected to a battery (not seen) and a voltmeter (bottom centre). The amount of hydrogen and oxygen gas produced in the voltmeter is a measure of the amount of electricity used. Chlorine is produced at the positive electrode (wire) and tin at the negative electrode (round coil). Weighing the coil showed that the amount of tin deposited was proportional to the amount of electricity. From *Physique Populaire* (E. Desbeaux, 1891). Science Photo library
23 Sep	Neptune. Science Photo Library
24 Sep	Everest summit. Doug Scott photographed by Dougal Haston after the pair had completed the first ascent of the formidable South West Face. He is standing beside the survey tripod planted by a previous Chinese expedition from the north – Tibetan – side of the mountain. John Cleare/Mountain Camera Picture Library
25 Sep	Statue of Sir Henry Havelock. Adam Swaine/Britain on View
26 Sep	The House in Stratford-upon-Avon in which Shakespeare was Born (engraving) (b&w photo) by R. Greene (19th century). Private Collection/Bridgeman Art Library
27 Sep	Duke William and his fleet cross the Channel to Pevensey, from the Bayeux Tapestry, before 1082 (wool embroidery on linen) (by French School (11th century). Musee de la Tapisserie, Bayeux, France/Bridgeman Art Library
28 Sep	H. Carey's 'God Save the King' score from early 18th century. Lebrecht Collection
29 Sep	Archangel Michael © Nicolette Caven 2007
30 Sep	Arthur Neville Chamberlain returns to the UK in 1938. Roger Viollet/Rex Features

Autumn tree	© Nicolette Caven 2007
Autumn	Cider Apples, 1899 (oil on canvas), La Thangue, Henry Herbert (1859–1929). Art Gallery of New South Wales, Sydney, Australia/Bridgeman Art Library
	The Football Match, 1890 (colour litho) by William Heysham Overend (1851–98). Private Collection/Bridgeman Art Library

October	The Rambler's Club, 1988, Lucy Rawlinson. Bridgeman Art Library/Getty Images
	Conn and Hal Iggulden at the World Conker Championships, 2006
1 Oct	Model T motor car, first produced by Ford in 1908. Three Lions/Getty Images
2 Oct	Richard III (1452–85) (oil on panel), English School, (16th century). Society of Antiquaries, London, UK/Bridgeman Art Library
3 Oct	Malhamdale Yorkshire Dales National Park, North Yorkshire, England/Robert Harding
4 Oct	St Francis of Assisi illo © Nicolette Caven 2007
5 Oct	A British army Gurkha soldier stands guard at the site of an apparent suicide attack while an Afghan woman passes by in the background in Kabul, 2004. Shah Marai/AFP/Getty Images

6 Oct	Captain Cook takes formal possession of New South Wales. Mary Evans Picture Library
7 Oct	The Spanish & Venetian fleets commanded by Don John of Austria. Mary Evans Picture Library
8 Oct	Poop! Poop! 1998 (oil on canvas) by Jonathan Barry (Contemporary Artist). Private Collection/Bridgeman Art Library
9 Oct	King Richard III and Aeneas, legendary founder of Warwick by Rous Roll. British Library /Art Archive
10 Oct	Poet John Betjeman reading on the train. Mark Kauffman//Time Life Pictures/Getty Images
11 Oct	James Joule (1818–1889), taken from *Physique Populaire*, 1891.
12 Oct	*The Book of Common Prayer*. In a contemporary binding, attributed to Richard Balley, of gold-tooled black morocco with red and citron onlays, and silver corner-mounts. British Library
13 Oct	Italian soldiers surrender in Sicily to place themselves under the jurisdiction of the Allies. Photo by Keystone/Getty Images
14 Oct	The Great Seal of England, 1651, the second seal used by the Commonwealth, showing the House in session, with the House of Commons. British Library, London, UK/Bridgeman Art Library
15 Oct	PG Wodehouse *Stiff Upper Lip, Jeeves*. Peter Harrington Antiquarian Bookseller
16 Oct	Battle of Waterloo, 1815, engraved by J.A. Cook, 1816 (coloured aquatint) by A. Sauerweld (fl.1816) (after). Courtesy of the Council, National Army Museum, London, UK/Bridgeman Art library
17 Oct	French troops outside a concrete pillbox which is the entrance to an underground fort in the Maginot line. Broderick/Keystone/Getty Images
18 Oct	A view looking across the Kunming Lake to the Summer Palace in former Peking (Beijing), c.1850. Hulton Archive/Getty Images
19 Oct	Battle of Zama, 202 BC, 1570–80 (oil on canvas) by Giulio Romano (1492–1546) Pushkin Museum, Moscow. Russia/Bridgeman Art Library
20 Oct	George I (1660–1727) by English School (18th century) © Bristol City Museum and Art Gallery, UK/Bridgeman Art Library
22 Oct	John F. Kennedy. Getty Images
23 Oct	British Prime Minister Winston Churchill addressing the 4th Hussars in Egypt. Popperfoto
24 Oct	On the left Vidkun Quisling (1887–1945) Norwegian diplomat and fascist leader. He is with Heinrich Himmler (1900–1945), head of the SS on a trip to Berlin. Three Lions/Getty Images
25 Oct	Battle of Agincourt, 1415, English with Flemish illuminations. Lambeth Palace Library, London, UK/Bridgeman Art Library
26 Oct	Gunfight at the OK Corral, 1957. Kirk Douglas, Burt Lancaster. Ronald Grant Archive
27 Oct	Dylan Thomas in his writing shed at The Boat House, Laugharne, 1953 (his arm in plaster after an accident in New York). Mary Evans Picture Library
28 Oct	Harvard University, Cambridge, from *Historical Collections of Massachusetts*, by John Warner Barber. Private Collection/Bridgeman Art Library
29 Oct	*Daily Mail* October 1929. John Frost Newspaper Collection
30 Oct	Family tree © Graeme Andrew

31 Oct	Up Helly Aa Lerwick, Shetlands, Scotland Celebration. Guy Somerset/Alamy
November	An unidentified early car race, with a cannon used instead of a starting flag. Original artwork. Look and Learn Magazine Ltd/Bridgeman Art Library
	Guy Fawkes (1570–1606) is arrested whilst attempting to blow up the Houses of Parliament Hulton Archive/Getty Images
	Branch illo © Joy Gosney 2007
1 Nov	Virgin Mary with the Apostles and Other Saints by Fra Angelico. The National Gallery, London
2 Nov	British Explorer Sir Ranulph Fiennes finishes his fifth marathon. Martin Hayhow/AFP/Getty Images
3 Nov	Laika the space dog postcard. Detlev van Ravenswaay/Science Photo Library
5 Nov	'Please to remember the fifth of November, The Gunpowder treason plot; I see no reason why Gunpowder treason, should ever be forgot. A stick and a stake for Victoria's sake!' Mary Evans Picture Library
6 Nov	The supremely efficient Hawker Hurricane as it appears at the outbreak of World War I – less glamorous than the 'Spitfire' but in practice the more effective aircraft © Mary Evans Picture Library
7 Nov	Artist's impression of the Mars Global Surveyor (MGS) spacecraft in orbit around Mars. Julian Baim/Science Photo Library
8 Nov	Halley's Comet in the night sky, artwork. Detlev van Ravenswaay/Science Photo Library
9 Nov	King Edward VII as Prince of Wales (1841–1910), portrait photograph by Stanislas Walery. Stapleton Collection, UK/Bridgeman Art Library
10 Nov	The Meeting of Stanley (1840–1904) and Livingstone (1813–73) at Ujiji, from Livingstone and the Explorate by English School (19th century). Royal Geographical Society
11 Nov	Graves and headstones for World War I and II soldiers at The National Cemetery. Lee Snider/Photo Images/Corbis
12 Nov	Troops loading a 400lb Cookie bomb onto a Lancaster Bomber. Hulton Archive/Getty Images
13 Nov	Portrait of Edward III (1312–77) from *Memoirs of the Court of Queen Elizabeth*, published in 1825. Getty Images
14 Nov	Coventry Cathedral, West Midlands, in ruins following a night-time attack by German bombers. Fox Photos/Getty Images
15 Nov	The Stone of Scone or Stone of Destiny captured by Edward I in 1296 and taken to London. Mary Evans Picture Library
16 Nov	An illustration of the planet Venus. Science Photo Library
17 Nov	The Tower of London, from a survey made in 1597 by W. Haiward and J. Gascoyne (engraving) by English School (19th century). Stapleton Collection, UK/Bridgeman Art Library
18 Nov	The Panama Canal © Popperfoto
19 Nov	American President Abraham Lincoln (1809–1865) raises his hand as he delivers the Gettysburg Address. The image was published as part of the 'Life of Lincoln' series by the C.W. Briggs Company. George Eastman House/Getty Images
20 Nov	Princess Elizabeth, and Prince Philip, Duke of Edinburgh at Buckingham Palace after their wedding. Hulton Archive/Getty Images

21 Nov	Workers with digging spades at the Piltdown Site in 1911. Nils Jorgensen/Rex Features
22 Nov	President John F. Kennedy rides in a motorcade with his wife Jacqueline, right, Nellie Connally, left, and her husband, Gov. John Connally of Texas in Dallas, Texas, file photo, prior to President Kennedy's assassination. AP
23 Nov	Early mainland letter box made in Gloucester c.1853. Located at Barnes Cross. Royal Mail Group/Mary Evans Picture Library
24 Nov	Gatling gun. Mary Evans Picture Library
25 Nov	Original poster from *The Mousetrap* at the Ambassadors Theatre, 1952
26 Nov	The gold mask, from the Treasure of Tutankhamun (c.1370–52 BC) c.1340 BC (gold inlaid with semi-precious stones). Egyptian National Museum, Cairo, Egypt/Giraudon/Bridgeman Art Library
27 Nov	c.1600, English playwright and poet William Shakespeare (1564–1616). Stock Montage/Getty Images
28 Nov	The Tyger: plate 43 from *Songs of Innocence and of Experience* (copy R) c.1802–08 (etching, ink and w/c) by William Blake (1757–1827). Bridgeman Art Library
29 Nov	St Edmund King and Martyr, Stained Glass Window, 1868, by C.E. Kempe. Staplefield Church, Sussex, UK/Bridgeman Art Library
30 Nov	St Andrew illo © Nicolette Caven 2007
December	Tree in Town Square. Mary Evans Picture Library
1 Dec	Tunnelling teams from Britain and France meet during the building of the Channel Tunnel when the final underground section between the Kent coast and the terminal site broke through. The workers are pictured celebrating their arrival in Folkstone. David Giles/PA Photos
2 Dec	Portrait of Sir Christopher Wren by Anonymous. Private Collection/Bridgeman Art Library
3 Dec	South African surgeon Dr Christiaan Barnard (1922–2001) performing a heart transplant on a dog at La Paz Hospital in Madrid, in order to demonstrate his methods. The dog died after the operation. Central Press/Getty Images
4 Dec	Suttee, 1831 (oil on canvas), James Atkinson (1780–1852). British Library, London/Bridgeman Art Library
5 Dec	The 100-foot Mary Celeste. A wood engraving by Rudolph Ruzicaka. Keystone/Getty Images
6 Dec	St Nicholas illo © Nicolette Caven 2007
7 Dec	360 Japanese war planes make a surprise attack on the US Pacific Fleet at Pearl Harbor, declaring war on the US and Britain. Mary Evans Picture Library
8 Dec	Paul McCartney, John Lennon, Ringo Starr, George Harrison performing 'From Me to You'. David Redfern/Redferns
10 Dec	Mowgli holds aloft the hide of Shere Khan. Illustration by J.M. Gleeson in *Outing* Vol 49, December 1906 Between p288 & p289. Author: Rudyard Kipling. Mary Evans Picture Library
11 Dec	King Edward VIII (1894–1972) and his brothers George (1895–1952) Duke of York and Henry Duke of Gloucester walk behind the gun carriage that carries their father, King George V in the royal funeral procession. Central Press/Getty Images

12 Dec	Napoleon Bonaparte (1769–1821) as Lieutenant Colonel of the 1st Battalion of Corsica, 1834 (oil on canvas), Felix Philippoteaux (c.1815–84). Chateau de Versailles, France/Bridgeman Art Library
13 Dec	The ship of Sir Francis Drake, formerly named *Pelican*. Mary Evans Picture Library
14 Dec	Memento on the Moon. The commemorative plaque, left behind on the Moon by the *Apollo 17* mission in December 1972. NASA/Science Photo Library
15 Dec	*Gemini 6A* launch. Officially known as *Gemini VI-A*. Inside were US astronauts Wally Schirra and Thomas Stafford. NASA/Science Photo Library
16 Dec	Designs for the programme for *Pride and Prejudice* featuring a shot of the book, produced at St. James's Theatre, February 1936 (pen, ink and w/c) by Rex Whistler (1905–44). Roy Miles Fine Paintings/Bridgeman Art Library
17 Dec	Beaufort Scale Depiction. National Meteorological Library and Archive
18 Dec	Nobel Prize Medal Bearing Likeness of Alfred Nobel. Ted Spiegel/Corbis.
19 Dec	*The Fighting Temeraire*. Tugged to her Last Berth to be Broken up, 1839 by Joseph Mallord William Turner (1775–1851). National Gallery, London, UK/Bridgeman Art Libary
20 Dec	Map showing the area covered by the Louisiana Purchase. MPI/Getty Images
21 Dec	Solstice illo © Joy Gosney 2007
22 Dec	Prince James Francis Edward Stewart (1688–1766), Anonymous. Scottish National Portrait Gallery, Edinburgh, Scotland/Bridgeman Art Library
23 Dec	Portrait of James II (1633–1701) in Garter Robes (oil on canvas) by Sir Peter Lely (1618–80). Bolton Museum and Art Gallery, Lancashire, UK/Bridgeman Art Library
24 Dec	England's King John (seated) signing the Magna Carta at Runnymede. In fact, he used a Royal seal to mark the document and did not sign his name. Mansell/Time Life Pictures/Getty Images
25 Dec	Triumphant return of Mr Christmas. Mary Evans Picture Library
26 Dec	St Stephen illo © Nicolette Caven
27 Dec	HMS *Beagle* in the Murray Narrows, Beagle Channel (w/c on paper) by Conrad Martens (1801–78). Down House, Kent, UK/Bridgeman Art Library
28 Dec	Ms 6712 (A.6.89) fol.123v William I (1028–87) the Conqueror, miniature from 'Flores Historiarum', by Matthew Paris, 1250–52 (by English School. Chetham's Library, Manchester, UK/Bridgeman Art library
29 Dec	Cask containing the remains of Thomas à Becket (c.1118–70), c.1190 (gold, lapis lazuli & semi-precious stones). Private Collection/Bridgeman Art Library
30 Dec	Grigori Rasputin. Mary Evans Picture Library
31 Dec	Hogmanay fireworks over Stirling Castle, Scotland. David Robertson

Did you miss the Galaxy Book Awards Book of the Year?

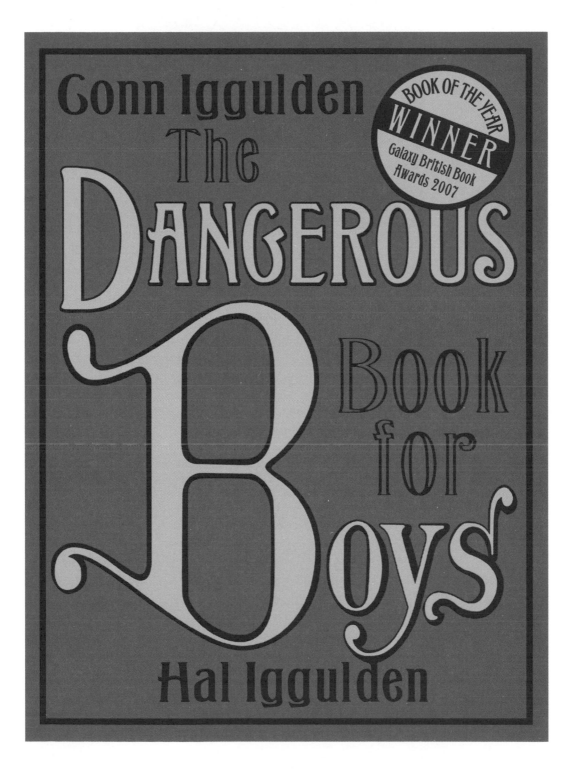

Out Now.
The new bestseller.

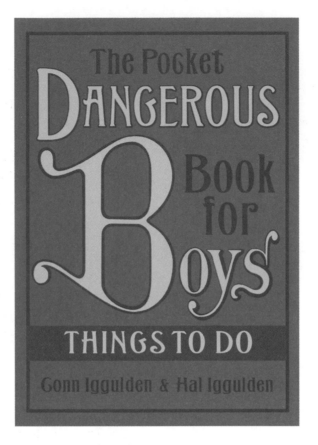

Coming in Summer 2008
The Pocket Dangerous Book for Boys: Things to Know

The Dangerous Book for Boys inspired a newfound passion for adventure, fun and all things 'dangerous'. To go alongside *The Pocket Dangerous Book for Boys: Things to Do* is a companion book, *The Pocket Dangerous Book for Boys: Things to Know*. Available in 2008, it is a compendium of the authors' facts: fun and frivolous, entertaining and useful.

Impress your friends and family with your amazing knowledge of the solar system, your uncanny ability to name the kings and queens of England, your breathtaking brilliance at unravelling codes and ciphers. *The Pocket Dangerous Book for Boys: Things to Know* will make every man and boy as knowledgeable as he has always wished to be!

ISBN 978 0 00 725401 9

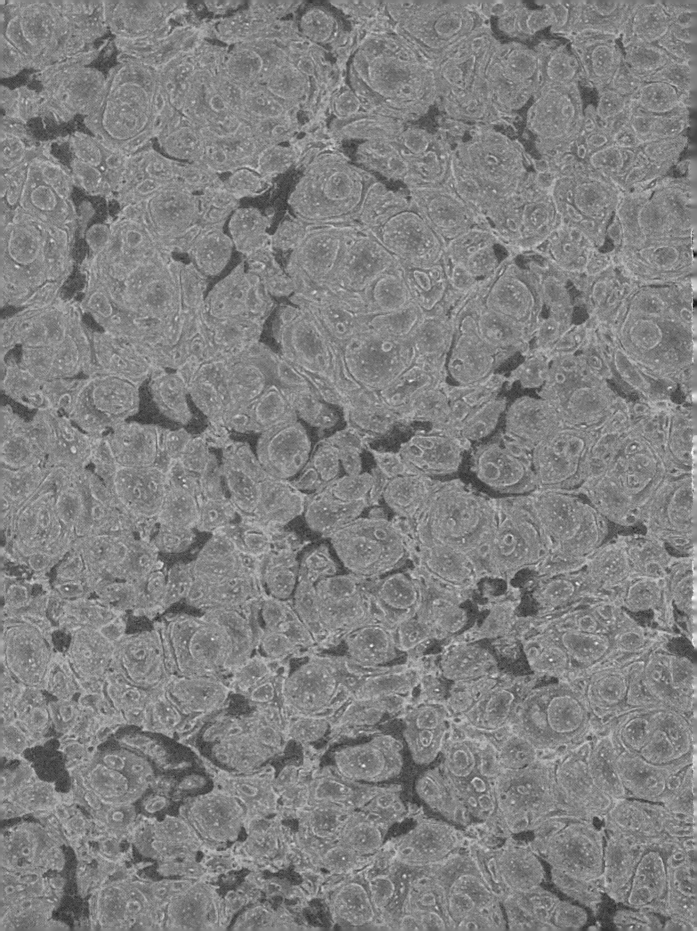